Science and the Question of Human Equality

AAAS Selected Symposia Series

 Published by Westview Press, Inc.
5500 Central Avenue, Boulder, Colorado

for the

 American Association for the Advancement of Science
1776 Massachusetts Avenue, N.W., Washington, D.C.

Science and the Question of Human Equality

Edited by
Margaret S. Collins, Irving W. Wainer,
and Theodore A. Bremner

AAAS Selected Symposium **58**

AAAS Selected Symposia Series

This book is based on a symposium which was held at the 1979 AAAS National Annual Meeting in Houston, Texas, January 3-8. The symposium was sponsored by AAAS Section G (Biological Sciences).

Published in 1981 in the United States of America by
  Westview Press, Inc.
  5500 Central Avenue
  Boulder, Colorado 80301
  Frederick A. Praeger, Publisher

Library of Congress Cataloging in Publication Data
Main entry under title:
Science and the question of human equality.
  (AAAS selected symposium ; 58)
    1. Race--Congresses. 2. Nature and nurture--Congresses. 3. Human
genetics--Congresses. 4. Ethnopsychology--Congresses. I. Collins,
Margaret S. II. Wainer, Irving W. III. Bremner. IV. Series: American
Association for the Advancement of Science. AAAS Selected Symposium ; 58.
GN269.S39   572   80-26969
ISBN 0-89158-952-X

Printed and bound in the United States of America

About the Book

This book provides an interdisciplinary look at racism and science, investigating the biological and social realities of individual and group differences. The contributors examine race and racial distinctions, environmental versus genetic contributions to IQ and to cognitive skill level, the impact of biocultural interactions on behavior, and the problems of achieving an objective appraisal of inter- and intragroup differences in humans. They also consider a possible model for cultural and biological evolution, recommending a careful selection of models and methods of approach for sciences concerned with the study of man. The book includes recent findings in the area of race and IQ, documents instances of racism and classism, and analyzes factors underlying these phenomena.

About the Series

The *AAAS Selected Symposia Series* was begun in 1977 to provide a means for more permanently recording and more widely disseminating some of the valuable material which is discussed at the AAAS Annual National Meetings. The volumes in this *Series* are based on symposia held at the Meetings which address topics of current and continuing significance, both within and among the sciences, and in the areas in which science and technology impact on public policy. The *Series* format is designed to provide for rapid dissemination of information, so the papers are not typeset but are reproduced directly from the camera-copy submitted by the authors. The papers are organized and edited by the symposium arrangers who then become the editors of the various volumes. Most papers published in this *Series* are original contributions which have not been previously published, although in some cases additional papers from other sources have been added by an editor to provide a more comprehensive view of a particular topic. Symposia may be reports of new research or reviews of established work, particularly work of an interdisciplinary nature, since the AAAS Annual Meetings typically embrace the full range of the sciences and their societal implications.

WILLIAM D. CAREY
Executive Officer
American Association for
the Advancement of Science

Contents

About the Editors and Authors

Margaret S. Collins *is a professor of zoology at Howard University in Washington, D.C. Her specialty is insect ecology and she has published widely in her field.*

Irving W. Wainer *is a research associate in pharmacology at Thomas Jefferson University in Philadelphia. His specialty is pharmacokinetics and clinical pharmacology, and he has written on the history of the concept of race, sociobiology and genetic engineering.*

Theodore A. Bremner *is an assistant professor of zoology at Howard University. He is a specialist in biochemical genetics.*

Marietta Lynn Baba *is adjunct associate professor of anthropology at Wayne State University. A physical anthropologist by training, her areas of interest are primate evolution, molecular evolution, human biology, urban culture and redevelopment.*

Robert Boyd *is an assistant professor in the School of Forestry and Environmental Studies at Duke University. His primary interest is in the evolutionary theory of human and animal social behavior.*

Linda L. Darga *is an NIH post-doctoral fellow at Children's Hospital in Detroit; she is a specialist in molecular anthropology and human variability.*

Rena C. Gropper, *an associate professor of anthropology at Hunter College, City University of New York, is a specialist in applied medical anthropology.*

John H. Moore, *an ethnologist, is associate professor of anthropology at the University of Oklahoma. He has published on race and racism and on American culture.*

Peter J. Richerson *is an associate professor in the Institute of Ecology at the University of California-Davis. His research interests are in ecology, especially in plankton communities, and in the application of ecological and evolutionary theory to humans.*

Sandra Scarr *is a professor of psychology at Yale University. Her areas of interest include developmental psychology, intelligence and behavior genetics. She is the author of* IQ: Race, Social Class and Individual Differences, New Studies of Old Problems *(Erlbaum, in press) and is editor of* Developmental Psychology.

Stephen L. Zegura *is an associate professor of anthropology and genetics at the University of Arizona. His specialties are physical anthropology, human biology and human genetics, and he is editor of* Eskimos of Northwestern Alaska: A Biological Perspective *(Dowden, Hutchinson & Ross, 1978).*

Acknowledgments

The editors wish to express appreciation to the Publications staff at AAAS, to the various reviewers of the manuscript for their constructive criticism of the volume as a whole, and to Dr. Arthur Caplan for his critical appraisal of one of the manuscripts.

Science and the Question of Human Equality

Margaret S. Collins, Irving W. Wainer,
Theodore A. Bremner

Introduction

The papers included in this volume are a contribution to
the continuing nature/nurture controversy. They represent
in part the record of a symposium entitled "Biology, Culture
and Human Evolution" held at the 1979 annual meeting of the
American Association for the Advancement of Science in Houston, Texas. Since the time of their presentation, the papers
have undergone substantial revision, and have been augmented
with others so that a change of title seemed appropriate.

The AAAS is the best forum for the critical analysis of
the gene-environment controversy because it comprises individuals competent in all the major social and scientific disciplines, many of whom influence the formulation or execution
of social policy, either directly or indirectly. It is precisely the concern that social policy will be influenced profoundly by its resolution that lends urgency and topicality
to the issue.

Our aim in bringing together this panel of investigators
was not merely to generate controversy for its own sake, but,
realizing the complexity of the issue, to create a context
within which relevant material could be presented and analyzed from a variety of scientific perspectives, so that our
analysis would be synoptic. It is our conviction that many
of the misconceptions about human nature masquerading as scientific fact result not so much from malign intent as from
methodological narrowness, a narrowness characteristic of
those who generalize limited, conditional truths into perma-
nent ordinances of nature.

There are those, however, who would argue that discussions such as these are pointless, the kind of research which
they generate is intrinsically biased, and therefore of dub-
ious worth. Such matters, it is felt, are best left alone.

1

Ironically, much of our world is already organized on the
basis of biology, or to put it more accurately, a folk biology remarkably similar to some of the assertions of eminent
scientists who argue that the stratifications and institutional arrangements of contemporary society are merely the
working out of a biologically determined plan. That the capacity for culture (the neurophysiological basis of human
behavior) is genetically determined seems a reasonable proposition, but to contend that any specific pattern of socially purposeful behavior is genetically determined (and, by implication, immutable) or, further, that the disparities in
contemporary society are reflective of disparities in the
genetic endowments of its participants is an assertion which
is not only unsupported by the scientific evidence, but also
too far-reaching in its social and political implications to
go unchallenged. Any gentlemen's agreement not to press the
issue is an agreement to leave the status quo alone, and to
give it a legitimacy which it may not deserve.

This book considers the biological and social realities
of individual and group differences. The questions of race
and racial distinctions; environmental versus genetic contributions to IQ and cognitive skill level; the impact of biocultural interactions on behavior; the problems faced in a-
chieving an objective appraisal of inter-and intra-group
differences in man; and a possible model for cultural and
biological evolution in man are considered by a group of individuals from a variety of disciplines.

Among the chief conclusions documented by contributors
to the volume are:

1. Differences between individuals within subgroups of
Homo sapiens are, on the average, of greater magnitude
than differences between the sub-groups.

2. Cultural practices may influence biological evolution.

3. IQ and cognitive skill level are highly malleable
traits and there is no justification for regarding
differences in levels demonstrable between samples
of Black and White populations as due to genetic
differences in potential of the members of the groups.

4. Recurring cycles of racism and classism in Anthropology reflect the influence of culture on the ideas
and models proposed by scientists; such ideas pervade both academic and leisure-time activities. The
training of students in sciences devoted to the study
of man provides a cognitive screen leading ultimately

to selective perception and, frequently, to confirmation of presuppositions which are then taught as facts.

5. Care should be exercised in selection of models and methods of approach to problems in sciences directed toward the study of man.

Whether our current social status is the result of historical accident or biological necessity is a question of over-riding importance. It is one of those "ultimate" questions which will not dissolve if we simply concentrate on penultimate ones. This question will not be answered simply. But, if our symposium accomplishes nothing more than a clarification of the question, or a broadening of the context within which it is discussed, we will have succeeded in our endeavor.

Marietta Lynn Baba, Linda L. Darga

1. The Genetic Myth of Racial Classification

Introduction

The classification of living and non-living things is a fundamental component of the human thought process and one of the major organizing principles of all human languages. Our propensity for classifying objects is part of the legacy of our earliest human ancestors.

The first humans, hunters and gatherers who directly confronted raw environmental forces, found their very survival linked to the understanding of differences between and similarities among natural objects and phenomena. Survival relied upon rapid identification of poisonous plants, sources of water, areas of shelter, and upon discrimination between friend and foe. Since the natural world is comprised of literally billions of different objects, the ability to analyze that world quickly was a function of the mental ability to compare and contrast objects, group them into their appropriate classes, and plan action appropriate to the classification. Likewise, human communication systems would be inoperative without a basic consensus of categorization within the speech community. The success of a hunting venture will depend upon the mutual expectation that each hunter is referring to the same animal. A system of classifying phenomena shared by a particular group of people is called a "folk taxonomy."

Just as early humans invented folk taxonomies to help them survive and communicate with each other, modern scientists have invented taxonomic systems to assist them in analyzing the universe and in communicating with their colleagues. In science, classifications serve a number of purposes. Like folk taxonomies, those of science aim to accomplish "economy of memory" (summarizing information and attaching convenient labels to it) and ease of manipulation which also became affixed to the designated people. For example, a "black fellow" in Elizabethan England was not a Negro but an untrustworthy and dangerous person. Western people viewed black skin as not only ugly, but as a "symbol of moral taint and turpitude" (Montagu 1942). Negroes were supposedly the descendants of Old Testament Ham, who had been physically marked by God as a punishment. Non-western cultures also categorize other peoples, but on the basis of different characteristics. For example, Chinese artists select height and curly hair as the distinguishing marks of European ancestry and may fail to note any color difference between themselves and Europeans (Sokal 1977). Brazilian folk taxonomy of human types, on the other hand, utilizes the outward manifestations of wealth and education as primary criteria of placement in different "races" and such considerations often outweigh those of skin color, hair form or facial features (Harris 1970).

We would expect that folk taxonomies developed in several societies would differ both in criteria of classification and in the number of categories recognized. Folk taxonomies grow out of cultural experience and their reflection of that experience is as varied as the cultures they are part of.

One characteristic which does seem to unite folk taxonomies is that typically they are not rigid or static. Sociocultural and political imperatives often demand that boundaries be vague so that persons can transfer out of one category and into another. In New York City, some Puerto Rican youths may "choose" their racial status by adopting appropriate speech mannerisms, friendships and values (Wolfram 1974); in several American Indian cultures "aliens" could be adopted through ritual to become part of the "people;" in Brazil, "money whitens" (Harris 1970).

Since Linnaeus published his General System of Nature in 1806, the scientific community has made numerous attempts to develop a classification system for Homo sapiens. There is nothing inherently good or evil in such attempts, since the incredible variety of H. sapiens demands analysis and explanation. But there are problems inherent in the development and utilization of such a classification. The very fact that such taxonomists are members of cultures means that their perceptions of human groups have historically been colored by their culture's perception of human differences. This means that the structure of racial folk taxonomies has often influenced the structure of scientific classifications. Furthermore, since the scientific taxonomies have been influenced by the folk taxonomies, the former have often not been able to fulfill their primary scientific objective, i.e., reflecting

evolutionary relationships and generating hypotheses about
the origin and maintenance of the groupings. This will be
explored later in the paper.

Even more troublesome than the development of a scientific system of human classification is the question of the
uses to which such systems are put. There has been a pro-
nounced tendency for certain forces within the cultural environment to attempt to render the racial taxonomies more profound than the actual meaning and purpose of any taxonomy
would warrant. Scientific attempts to classify human populations on the basis of physical differences always link physical distinctions to differences in genetic material. If the
taxonomies are then used in society for purposes beyond their
legitimate field of meaning, the genetic basis of classification takes on enormous social and political importance. The
uses and abuses of scientifically proposed racial taxonomies
will also be reviewed in this paper.

Problems in the Development and Use of Racial Taxonomies

The most important functions of human classification
include economy of memory, ease of manipulation and reflection of natural laws (Sokal 1977). The latter criterion is
critical if the taxonomy is to serve as a mechanism for
generating hypotheses about the origin and maintenance of
classes of objects found in nature. Racial taxonomies have
generally failed to perform the expected functions, however,
and their utility in the pursuit of knowledge about the
human species is questionable.

A. Economy of Memory

Racial classifications have not afforded the scientific
community "economy of memory," i.e., summarizing information
and attaching convenient labels to each summary statement.
There has been no agreement among human biologists on the
number of races that exist, the groups to be included in
each race, the criteria to be used for categorization, or
the labels to affixed to each group.

Immanuel Kant began the racial numbers game in 1775
when he denoted four human varieties (Whites, Negros,
Mongolian and Hindu). By Darwin's time there was great dis-
agreement about the number of races that existed, with various authors suggesting the correct number to be two (Virey)
three (Jacquinot), five (Blemenbach), six (Buffon), seven
(Hunter), eight (Agassiz), eleven (Pickering), fifteen (Bory
St. Vincent) sixteen (Desmoulins), 22 (Morton), 60 (Crawford)
and 63 (Burke) (Darwin 1871). The debate continues today

with modern authors suggesting five (Coon 1962), six (Boyd 1950) eight (Brues 1977) and "just over two dozen" races (Goldsby 1971).

Garn, in Human Races (1965), attempted to solve the problem of how many races exist by creating three levels of racial classification: Geographic races which are coincident with continental boundaries and are few in number; local races which equal breeding units and could rise to several hundred; and microraces which occur because of isolation by numbers, i.e., the denser the population the closer you marry. This solution merely increases the number of racial categories ad infinitum.

Obviously the set of criteria one selects as the basis for distinguishing human groupings is directly related to the number and kind of groupings one discovers. Linnaeus (1806) used not only skin color, facial form and body build, but also judgments of moral and intellectual quality to define racial groupings. One hundred-fifty years later, Boyd (1950) added a new type of criterion--frequency of blood group antigens. The inclusion of blood group data was significant because it was hoped that "objective" tabulations of such quantitative characteristics would produce a racial classification more scientifically valid than the more subjective, non-quantitative, differences in morphology used earlier. But the use of gene frequencies opens whole new areas of debate--which gene frequencies are to be used? Should gene frequencies for sickle cell anemia, lactase deficiency and PTC testing be included? There are hundreds of different genetic loci that could be considered, and each requires a separate subdivision of the human species. The view that race must be determined by examining the "boundaries of natural breeding units" (Howells 1959) led to further confusion; since gene flow unites all human populations, was a race one population or a cluster of populations?

Since each proposed classification has a different set of assumptions and different groupings of taxa, it is not surprising that the labels attached to each "race" vary widely. Thus, a person of African descent could be a Negro, an Ethiopian or a Congoid-Capoid, depending upon which authority one consulted. Certainly such chaos in categories, criteria, and labels fails to provide "economy of memory." This "confusion of communication" stems from the profound difficulty inherent in attempting to segregate a continuously varying species into a finite set of rigidly bounded categories. As Darwin himself noted in 1971, the "diversity in judgment (about how many races exist) shows that they graduate into each other, and that it is hardly possible to discover clear distinctive characters between them" (Darwin 1871).

B.   Ease of Manipulation

A related problem of the racial approach to human variability is its failure to provide "ease of manipulation." By this we mean that scientific classifications ought to facilitate comparison and contrast of their component classes, enabling the investigator to determine relationships among groups more easily. In a classification of nonhuman primates, for example, the use of biological traits as criteria for inclusion in various categories also facilitates drawing evolutionary conclusions about the resulting groups. But in racial taxonomies, the use of biological traits for classification has failed to cluster populations into readily comparable units.

Heirnaux (1964) looked for racial groupings within Africa by clustering populations based on similarities and differences in frequency of several traits such that the distances between populations within the same group were less than the intergroup (inter-race) distances. No matter how he tried to group the populations he used, no clearcut clusters, or "races," emerged, and he concluded that a useful classification could not be developed for these populations. He also pointed out that this amount of variability is not peculiar to Africa.

One source of the difficulty in defining races and assigning populations to them stems from the fact that the natural distribution of most human variation is geographically continuous. For example, the distribution of blood type B in Europe ranges from a low of 0-5% in Spain to 25-30% in northern Russia (Mourant 1954). Such clinal distributions of traits defy grouping populations into rigid categories. To make the situation even more complex, clines for different traits seem to have their own unique slope and direction. Thus, the cline for melanin concentration in Europe increases from north to south, cross-cutting the cline for the blood type B allele; that is, variation is discordant. Any human population living at one particular point in space is thus crisscrossed by several intersecting clines. This complex situation is produced by continuous gene flow within the species and is not amenable to simple classificatory schemes. Thus as Heirnaux discovered for Africa, a group of populations that cluster for one set of traits will not remain together if other traits are added to the analysis. The groupings will always be arbitrary, which renders their comparison and contrast impossible.

Arbitrary clustering of populations is a conceptual error derived from typological thinking. Carlton Coon (1965) proposing five major races, exemplifies the typological approach. Each race is described by a laundry list of traits as though this listing represented an ideal type. Just as all Neandertals were thought to look like the type specimen of the Old Man of La Chapelle, all members of a racial group are thought to approximate his idealization. The egregious results of a typological approach to biological variability have been discussed eloquently by Mayr (1963 and later articles) among others.

For the human species the typological approach violates any attempt to understand the extent of the variability that actually exists. Since variant forms of a trait are not geographically restricted specific racial groups, one cannot understand the origin and distribution of sickle cell trait, for instance, by looking only at a so-called Negroid race.

C.   Theoretical Sterility

The final, but most serious, failure of racial taxonomies is their theoretical sterility. Scientific taxonomies should reflect the operation of nature's laws and thus provide an impetus for the generation of hypotheses about the order which has been described.

Although the history of racial taxonomies is rich with hypotheses generated to explain the origins and maintenance of variability, the bulk of these hypotheses have not been worthy of scientific scrutiny. For example, many racial origins hypotheses presented in the 18th and 19th centuries were frankly undisguised apologies for colonial exploitation and enslavement of colonial peoples (Ashley Montagu 1974). Such hypotheses explained the emergence of population differences as a process producing a hierarchical ranking among the groups observed. The Polygenic theory of race held that human races were not races at all, but entirely different species. Haeckel (1868) noted that "if Negroes and Caucasians were snails, zoologists would universally agree that they represented two very different species, which could never have originated from one pair by gradual divergence." The principle evidence in support of this hypothesis was the supposed finding that the offspring of Negro and Causasian unions were less fertile than offspring of matings within either group.

Species differences between these races encompassed more than anatomy and physiology, but extended to innate

intellectual and temperamental differences as well. Native
Americans were "averse to cultivation, and slow in acquiring
knowledge; restless, revengeful and fond of war...," Negroes
were "joyous, flexible and indolent" and represented the
"lowest grade" of hominid forms (Gossett 1963). Other
authors went still further in the conclusions they drew.
Nott and Gliddon (1854) in their eight volumn Types of Mankind (which ran through nine editions) noted that no Negro,
Indian or other person of color could display evidence of
intellect unless they had at least one white ancestor.
Indians could not be civilized, "...you might as well try to
change the nature of a buffalo;" Negroes were closer to the
chimpanzee and the orangutan than they were to Caucasians.
Finally, "...dark-skinned races, history attests, are only
fit for military government. It is the unique rule genial
to their physical nature: they are unhappy without it...."
The American Moncure Conway added that "The Caucasian race
is the highest species and that this supreme race has the
same right of dominion over the lower species of his genus
that he has over quadrupeds." (cf Stanton 1960).

Although the Monogenist school of thought held that all
humans were members of a single species, the varieties of
man were not equal. Since their arrival at the threshhold
of humanity some groups of humans had "degenerated" from
their originally "white state," and their descendants are
the colored peoples of the earth. History has demonstrated
the barren nature of these hypotheses. Today such theories
appear as contrived rationalizations for a priori judgments
(Haller 1971).

Racial taxonomies generated by colonial empires and
slavocracies must perform a specific social function--to
divide and order humanity in such a way that exploitation
and enslavement are not only justified, but even demanded.
Some in the rising science of physical anthropology lent
their credentials and methodology to the social and economic
issues of the day. Gould (1978) has shown how insidious was
the process by which scientific classifications were invaded
by the assumptions of pre-existent folk taxonomies. For
example, Samuel G. Morton, a 19th century naturalist, analyzed cranial capacities in order to show differences among
racial categories. Morton's analysis concluded that whites
were superior to Indians in intelligence and that Negroes
were at the bottom of the scale. Gould demonstrates that
Morton unconsciously manipulated his data in such a way as
to yield the culturally anticipated results. When his data
are reinterpreted without prejudice, all races have approximately equal capacities. Gould notes that "unconscious or
dimly perceived finagling is probably endemic in science

since scientists are human beings rooted in cultural contexts
not automatons directed toward eternal truth."

The theoretical sterility of racial classifications is
not limited to those produced by the 19th century. Twen-
tieth century racial taxonomies, although less obvious about
or totally innocent of discriminatory intent, are also im-
potent in furthering our understanding of human variation.
It is exemplary of the sterility of modern racial classifications to contrast the gigantic intellectual steps being
taken by the mainstream of evolutionary theory during the
first half of the 20th century (see Huxley's text Evolution:
the Modern Synthesis) with the intellectual paralysis experienced in physical anthropology at the same time (see
Hooten's text Up from the Apes). In those years before W.W.
II most physical anthropologists found themselves bound by a
theoretical perspective that stultified analysis of human
variability and slowed their application of the new knowledge of population genetics. Physical anthropologists were
unable to utilize the modern synthesis of evolutionary
theory which had emerged. The typological approach led to
the view that races were static and unchanging and that consequently, traits used to define them must be essentially
nonadaptive and not amenable to an evolutionary analysis.

By the 1950's and 1960's the previous view that races
were distinguished by nonadaptive traits faded and a rein-
troduction of fundamental evolutionary theory into physical
anthropology occurred. Despite gains in looking at certain
aspects of human diversity, however, some works again repeat
past failures. Coon (1968) for instance, pursues the evolutionary history of five races in his book, Origin of Races.
Though attempting to be more objective than his predecessors,
Coon leaves himself open to charges of racism by the evolutionary tack on which he chooses to portray the development
of his major "races." He asserts that modern races are
ancient and selectively uses the fossil record to present
evidence for a continuity of modern racial groups back
1,000,000 years, into the period of H. erectus. Each of the
races or subspecies then "crosses the sapient" independently.
From his reading of the fossil record, he argues that Europeans were the first to cross this threshhold followed by the
other four races, each at their own, slower, pace. Not only
is Coon unique among physical anthropologists in determining
that a single trait, cranial form and capacity, signals
attainment of a higher species distinction, but he seems
oblivious to the social connotations of his view of the
earlier mental and physical advancement of Europeans compared
with other races. One need not use the word "superiority"
to have the concept clearly embedded in one's work.[1]

Finally, Coon does look to human adaptation (1965) with at times eloquent hypotheses about the origin and maintenance of geographic variation in our species. However, when he questions the differences in skin color, nose shape, body build, etc., it is notable that he addresses the clinal variation in these traits and therefore is forced to transcend the very racial categories he spends so many pages constructing. In order to propose testable hypotheses about human variability, his racial classification is no longer scientifically useful.

Others (e.g., Hulse 1963) have attempted to apply the zoological concept of a subspecies to humans, thus attempting to cluster populations so that 75% of the members of one race can "unequivocally" be distinguished from members of another similar such cluster. With the proliferation of criticisms of a racial approach, use of a subspecies definition seems to offer more flexibility and to allow treatment of the human species much as zoologists were apparently treating other animal species. However, it is ironic that physical anthropologists attempted to apply the subspecies concept and this 75% threshold to humans at the very time that zoologists were abandoning the same approach for other species, realizing that clinal variation in most species renders subspecific boundaries vague or non-existent and leads to confusion. This approach seems most useful either where there are genetic isolates within a species or where lack of knowledge of the extent of variation within the species means subspecific designations are based on one or two traits only. Neither of these exceptions applies to the human species (Jolly and Plog 1976).

Today there seems less concern with constructing new racial systems (except see Brues 1977). With more fruitful approaches to human variability yielding important insights in understanding human differences, many have abandoned the older approach. (See newer texts in the field such as Weiss and Mann 1978; Jolly and Plog 1976.) Those who hang onto the concept of race or racial variation (e.g., see Stern 1971) define race, seemingly innocuously, as a geographic division of mankind whose gene pool differs from all other such divisions. This approach may avoid the numbers game, but in what way does it increase our understanding of human variability? It tells us that each human population has a different gene pool, but it does not explain what purpose is served by attempting to group these populations and then calling the groups "races;" nor how we can better understand the evolutionary relationships among these populations or "races".

In addition, just as the scientific racial classifications of the 18th and 19th centuries interfaced with the
racial folk classifications of the day, so racial classification today also serves a purpose in the larger social
context. Unfortunately, modern scientific classification of
humanity may offer reinforcement for folk taxonomies of
races which have been roundly attacked on legal and moral
grounds. In those cultures where caste and class systems
have effectively trapped peoples of color in the lowest
niches of the socioeconomic structure, scientific racial
classifications frequently leave the arena of science and
find varied uses in the political sphere. The "scientific"
notion that humanity may be divided into discrete categories
on the basis of genetic differences has effectively served
as a groundwork for arguments that: link race to differences
in performance on I. Q. tests (Jensen 1969); and further,
that remedial education can serve no purpose in improving
the learning capacity of certain groups of people when
learning limitations are set by genes; that intermarriage
between "races" is biologically dangerous to the species
and must be forbidden by law;[2] and even the somewhat comical
fear of receiving a blood transfusion from a member of another "race."

Perhaps the most dangerous social implication of scientifically proposed racial classification derives from the
power of their supposed genetic basis. While individuals
may "pass" through the boundaries of folk taxonomies by possessing or adopting a few superficial characteristics of
other racial groups, the genetically-based system allows no
such transfer. Since an individual cannot alter his or her
complement of genes, each person is assigned to one category
for all eternity.

The Genetic Myth of Racial Taxonomy

During the 1960's a profound revolution occurred in
genetics, biology, and anthropology. The revolution was
precipitated by the technological advances taking place in
electrophoretic and immunological techniques that finally
permitted detection of the individual variability occurring
in serum and tissue proteins and enzymes. These biological
traits were chosen for ease of laboratory analysis rather
than because they were already known to vary, as is the case
for traits chosen to demonstrate racial variation. Assay
of well over 20 protein systems in many different species
(see, for instance, Hubby and Lewontin 1965; Lewontin and
Hubby 1965; Darga et al. 1975; Harris 1970) yielded surprising results. In species as different as fruitflies and

humans, when 20 or more systems were investigated, a substantial number, often exceeding one-third of the traits
tested, were polymorphic within populations and subspecies.
This information came as quite a shock, since, for theoretical reasons related to such concepts as genetic load
(Lewontin 1974), it was assumed that any species could tol-
erate only a limited amount of genetic variability--far less
than the huge amount attested to by electrophoretic analysis
(Muller 1950; however, see Dobzhansky 1954). In evolutionary
theory one response was to look toward non-Darwinian evolution as an answer to the source and maintenance of this variability, representing a change in the conceptual framework
for looking at adaptation and evolution.

The effects of these important genetic discoveries on
the conceptual framework supporting a racial approach to
diversity should be equally dramatic. Traditionally, human
taxonomists have believed that members of the human species
approximate genetic homogeneity, except for those traits
assumed to be racial variants. (Traits such as skin color
and hair form have assumed undeserved importance since it is
thought that they represent significant differences among
groups. These are also the traits which we perceive most
readily and use in individual identification.) But now,
human variability is recognized to be extensive, both within
geographic groups and between them.

Most significantly, the new techniques which afford the
possibility of assessing within-group vs. between-group differences should demonstrate whether modern racial classifications, supposedly based on genetic differences, are valid.
Lewontin (1972) used 16 loci, including proteins and blood
group data, for which several human populations had been
assessed. He divided the populations into seven more or less
traditional racial categories: Caucasian, Africans, Mongol-
oids, South Asian Aborigines, Amerinds, Oceanians and Aus-
traliam Aborigines. With statistical techniques he appor-
tioned the genetic diversity into amounts found both within
and between populations assessed, and into the amount of
diversity found among his seven racial categories. The
results of Lewontin's analysis show that eighty-five per cent
of all genetic diversity occurred within populations; only
8% occurred among populations within races. The most star-
tling fact of all was that differences between traditional
racial categories accounted for only 6.3% of the variability
found.

Our view that genetic differences between races exceed
differences within them (a basis of all racial classifications) is erroneous. However, the racial bias is so

pervasive that we still must discuss geographic variation in humans as though it will somehow fit into racial categories.

Conclusion

Within a social context pervaded by the political and economic inequality of various national-ethnic groupings, some social forces are always anxious to render "scientific" racial taxonomies more profound than any taxonomy has a right to be rendered--to read meaning into a classification which was never intended by its author and for which there is no basis in fact. The epitome of such renderings is found in a statement by Juan Peron, late dictator of Argentina. On October 12, 1947, in a speech on the Day of Race, Peron said:

For us, race is not a biological concept. For us, it is something spiritual. It constitutes a sum of the imponderables that make us what we are and impel us to be what we should be, through our origin and through our destiny. It is that which dissuades us from falling into the imitation of other communities whose natures are foreign to us. For us, race constitutes our personal seal, indefinable and irrefutable. (cf. Ashley Montagu 1974)

This vision of race is appropriate to a folk taxonomy of human variation with dangerous social, political and moral implications. Although a "sum of imponderables" has no place in scientific classification, once created, racial taxonomies are publically available as receptacles for many of the myths that underpin social injustice.

The intricate patterns of genetic variability woven in the fabric of the human species cannot be framed in rigid, simplistic or static structure. We know that more variability occurs within human populations than between them. The sciences of human biology seem best advanced when we pose questions about particular types of variability within the framework of evolutionary mechanisms that affect all life forms. Without the operation of social forces to legitimize the folk taxonomy of discrimination, the concept of race in the biological sciences would have died long ago.

Notes

1. We might pause to note, after Coon's emphasis on cranial capacity as admitting some first into the species H. sapiens, a pair of pictures in Living Races of Man which illustrates a point he is making. He contrasts Topsey, a Tiwi woman to whom he attributes a cranial capacity of 1000 cc with a male Chinese scholar, to whom he attributes a cranial capacity of

2000cc, labeling them the "Alpha" and "Omega" of mankind,
respectively. This illustration should cause us to question
how objective a racial classification can be in our culture.

2. Ironically, it is the very myth of race, bolstered by racial taxonomies of scientific origin which is one of the primary mechanisms by which phenotypic differences between populations are maintained in most modern societies. The reification of an ideological construct called race restricts
gene flow and random mating between populations, inhibiting
the admixture that might otherwise render us racially indis-
tinguishable from one another.

References

1. B. Berlin, D.E. Breedlove & P.H. Raven, Principles of
    Tzeltal Plant Classification. New York: Academic Press,
    (1974).
2. J.F. Blumenbach, On the Natural Variety of Mankind.
    Doctoral Thesis. (Translated by T. Bendysshe, 1865)
    London, (1775).
3. W.C. Boyd, Genetics and the Races of Man. Boston:
    Little, Brown, (1950).
4. A.M. Brues, People and Races. New York: Macmillan,
    (1977).
5. C.S. Coon, The Living Races of Man. New York: Alfred A.
    Knopf, (1965).
6. C.S. Coon, The Origin of Races. New York: Alfred A.
    Knopf, (1968).
7. L.L. Darga, M. Goodman, M.L. Weiss, G.W. Moore, W.
    Prychodko, H. Dene, R. Tashian & A.L. Koen. In Isozymes
    IV. Genetics and Evolution. Ed. C.L. Markert. New
    York: Academic Press (1975).
8. C. Darwin, On the races of man. In This is Race. Ed.
    E.W. Count. New York: Henry Schuman, (1950) pp. 133-144.
9. T. Dobzhansky, Symposium of Quantitative Biology 20:1-15
    (1954).
10. S.M. Garn, Human Races. Springfield, Ill. Charles C.
    Thomas (1965).
11. R.A. Goldsby, Race and races. New York: Macmillan Co.
    (1971).
12. S.T. Gould, Human Variation 1(7):80-87 Also Science
    (1978).
13. T.F. Gossett, Race -- the history of an idea in America.
    Dallas: Southern Methodist University (1963).
14. E. Haeckel, The history of creation. In This is Race.
    Ed. E.W. Count. New York: Schuman, 1950, pp. 123-132
    (1968).
15. J.S. Haller, Jr. Outcasts from Evolution. Urbana:
    University of Illinois Press (1971).

18   Baba and Darga

16. H. Harris, The Principles of Human Biochemical Genetics. Amsterdam: North Holland Publication Co. (1970).
17. M. Harris Southwestern Journal of Anthropology 26(1): 1-13. (1970).
18. W. Hennig, Phylogenetic Systematics. Chicago: University of Chicago Press (1966).
19. J. Hiernaux, The concept of race and taxonomy of mankind. In The Concept of Race, Ed. M.F. Ashley Montagu. New York: Collier-Macmillan, (1964).
20. E.A. Hooten, Up From the Apes. 2nd Edition. New York: Macmillan, (1946).
21. W. Howells, Mankind in the Making. New York: Doubleday, (1959).
22. J.L. Hubby and R.C. Lewontin. Genetics 54:577-594, (1965).
23. F.S. Hulse, The Human Species. New York: Random House, (1963).
24. J.S. Huxley, Evolution, the Modern Synthesis. New York: Harper, (1942).
25. A.R. Jensen. Harvard Educational Review. Winter, 1969. pp. 1-123.
26. C.J. Jolly and F. Plog. Physical Anthropology and Archeology. New York: Alfred A. Knopf, Inc., (1976).
27. I. Kant. On the different races of man. In This is Race. Ed. E.W. Count. New York: Henry Schuman, 1950. pp. 16-24, (1775).
28. C. Kluckholn & D. Leighton. The Navaho. New York: Doubleday, (1962).
29. R.C. Lewontin. The apportionment of human diversity. In Evolutionary Biology Vol. VI. Eds. Th. Dobzhansky, M.K. Hecht & W.C. Steere. New York: Appleton, Century, Crofts, (1972).
30. R.C. Lewontin. The Genetic Basis of Evolutionary Change. New York: Appleton, Century, Crofts, (1972).
31. R.C. Lewontin. Genetics 54:595-609. (1965).
32. C. von. Linnaeus. A General System of Nature. London. (1806).
33. E. Mayr. Animal Species and Evolution. Cambridge, Mass. The Belknap Press (1963).
34. A. Montagu. Man's Most Dangerous Myth. London: Oxford University Press. (1974).
35. S.G. Morton. Crania Americana. Philadelphia. (1839).
36. A.E. Mourant. The Distribution of the Human Blood Groups. Oxford: Blackwell Scientific Publications. (1954).
37. H.J. Muller. American Journal of Human Genetics 2:111-176. (1950).
38. J.C. Nott & G.R. Gliddon. Types of Mankind. Philadelphia. (1854).
39. R.R. Sokal. Science 185(4157):1115-1123. (1977).

40. W. Stanton. The Leopard's Spots. Chicago: University of Chicago Press. (1960).
41. C. Stern. Genetic aspects of race. In Background for Man. Eds. P. Dolhinow & V.M. Sarich. Boston: Little, Brown & Co. (1971).
42. M.L. Weiss & A.E. Mann. Human Biology and Behavior. 2nd Edition. Boston: Little, Brown & Co. (1978).
43. G. Witherspoon. Language and Art in the Navaho Universe. Ann Arbor: University of Michigan Press. (1977).
44. W. Wolfram. Sociolinguistic Aspects of Assimilation. Arlington, Virginia: Center for Applied Linguistics. (1974).

2. The Myths of Cultural Anthropology

Anthropologists, like all human beings, are carriers of a culture and members of a society. As such, they share behavior, attitudes and values with other members of the sociocultural units into which they are born (1). These behaviors, attitudes and values are subject to change, of course, but they are laid down early in life and become an integral part of the individuals involved. The field of anthropology itself, although of international scope in terms of country of origin of its members, originated and developed within Euroamerican civilization. Thus, its accepted behaviors, attitudes and values tend to reflect those of Euroamerican peoples.

These values tend to assign high status to tangible items, such as machines and other material goods, and therefore to technology. The conversion sequence, manufacturing, originally a means to an end, becomes valued in itself. This leads to a positively valenced emphasis on altering and controlling as desirable activities and on "more" and "bigger" as "better." It also fosters increasing complexity and centralization, which in turn become hallmarks of excellence.

Our thought habits condition us to think in terms of opposing pairs: good vs. evil, man vs. woman, simple vs. complex, homogeneous vs. heterogeneous, isolated vs. interdependent, stable vs. changing, etc. (2). These dichotomies tend to imply either/or propositions rather than complementarities. "You are either for us or against us," we say; we do not refer to a balance between yin and yang.

For Westerners and especially for Americans, time is a thing (3). This reification has several consequences: time is not only measurable, but also divisible and storable. It can be cut, and it can be saved. It is finite, existing in

limited quantities, and it is irreversible. We say it can
be "used up" or "wasted." Conceptualization of time in processual terms, as a continuous flow and/or as perpetually
recurrent cycles does not come easily to us. The small
counterbalance afforded by farming, with its emphasis upon a
regular succession of seasons, has eroded with our increasing reliance on industrialization. Thus, we tend to refer
to "events," with a beginning and end, more often than to
"episodes," with a sense of recurrence. "The die is cast;"
"what is done cannot be undone," we affirm. We extrapolate
these attitudes to problem-solving, too. We expect that,
once found, a solution is final, that we shall not have to
face it again. "That's that," we announce with satisfaction.

   This kind of thinking makes it difficult for us to han-
dle flux despite all our emphasis on progress and change.
We tend to take stability as our base line, and we leap
from one stable point to another. Transitions are felt to
be chaotic, upsetting, and temporary. Again our linguistic
term indicates our discomfort -- transition period, with
the semantic overtone of equivalence to a point.

   The natural and social sciences also emerged from the
Euroamerican milieu and were nurtured in the same cultural
biases. I say this, knowing full well that scientists pride
themselves on the supposed international, universalistic
nature of their ways of thinking and working. Indeed, they
use the commonality of thinking and working as evidence of
the "truth" of their methods. What we scientists tend to
forget is that science education includes socialization into
the profession which is an indoctrination into values and
attitudes as well as into specifically scientific concepts
and methodology. These values and attitudes remain those
of the nurturing Euroamerican cultures. Thus, young scientists, no matter what their original sociocultural back-
grounds, undergo heavy pressures during the educational process to acculturate to Euroamerican culture. There is a
strong positive correlation between high degree of acceptance of Euroamerican values and future international ac-
claim as a scientist. I would argue further that the emphasis on observability, replication, and quantification,
so integral to our scientific method, stems from the high
value Euroamericans place on technology and machines. I
put it to you that a shared bias in thinking, no matter how
widely distributed through time and space, is not necessarily indicative of reality.

   Science training also includes socialization into a belief system. To become a scientist, one must learn and

accept fundamental assumptions that are necessary articles
of faith -- basic building blocks of our thinking, but not
testable. For instance, if we did not acknowledge at least
partial determinism in the universe, we could not refer to
cause-and-effect. We also believe that the universe has a
complex interrelationship of its parts and variables such
that consistencies and regularities exist, allowing us to
"understand" and "explain" phenomena. However, consistencies and regularities are approximations, not absolutes,
because the universe is a statistical one, we assert. This
constitutes a marvelous fallback position, allowing us to
point to conformity when we can and to invoke randomness
when we cannot. In what way is this type of explanation
different from that utilized by other groups when they
tell us that exact replication of ritual will produce au-
tomatic results -- unless inadvertent mistakes are made?

Our science emphasizes experimentation using controls.
Other cultures utilize data accumulation and knowledge improvement via experimentation, but without controls. (From
their viewpoint, the situation in existence prior to the
experimental manipulation is the control.) For example,
in many medical care systems involving herbalists, the cur-
ers search constantly for new plants which, when found, they
first try out on themselves to determine the physiological
effects. If the substance produces a discernible change,
the properties are duly noted and trial administration on
others occurs. If and when consistent results are obtained,
that plant is added to the pharmocopoeia.

We test out our theories and hypotheses; members of
many other cultures also collect evidence to check on the
hypotheses under which they operate. The Tibetan physi-
cians characteristically witnessed the dismemberment of a
deceased patient when they wanted to confirm a diagnosis or
to evaluate the treatment modality that had been used.

But I anticipate the protests: our science deals with
reality; the others deal with the nonexistent. How does one
recognize reality? "Description of a nonexistent phenomenon
or material from an authoritative laboratory may lead to
bona fide experimentation leading to confirmation of the
same nonexistent phenomenon" (4). Perhaps the reader would
like to argue that our explanations are contingent upon new
testing as ongoing procedure, but we do not always act as if
such were the case. Moreover, evidence is beginning to
emerge that other knowledge systems operate the same way.
For example, Carol Laderman, an anthropologist recently re-
turned from Malaysia, found that the people seem to have a
packet of possible hypotheses upon which they draw <u>post</u>

facto. She found that, contrary to earlier reports, the Ma-
lays function in a "maybe" and "sometimes" universe, not in
an absolute one (5). In how many other groups does this
exist without having been reported?

Our articles of faith are neither sacrosanct nor ac-
tualities. Nevertheless, like adherents to any set of beliefs, we "defend" them, treat them as reality, and consider
them superior to other belief systems. We even resent
their being classified as "belief systems."

The particular circumstances under which anthropologists have worked also molded the way we think. The foundations of our data base rest on fieldwork (6). Fieldwork
conditions are subject to many external constraints. The
traditional sphere of our investigations, a group of people
situated away from the place of our income-producing activities, necessitated an exaggerated separation of our professional lives into research and non-research components
in terms of both geographic space and calendric time. We
did our research during summer recess, or we obtained funds
to cover our expenses for a year or so. Transportation was
relatively slow as well as expensive, and travel time could
chew away six or more weeks from the total field period.
Dickering with officials for final arrangements, selection
of the specific field operations site, and arranging for
base headquarters and shelter all made additional inroads
into the actual research time. Learning the native language, mapping, censustaking, and collection of genealogies,
although a necessary part of fieldwork, were (and are) time-
consuming and yield comparatively little sophisticated data
without additional methodological supplementation. Therefore, real working time was (and is) further reduced. Because anthropologists were few in number and tribal groups
were changing or dying out, we felt obligated to return
with as complete a picture of the people as possible. We
conceded grudgingly that no one could do a complete report
of the human biology, archeology, linguistics, and cultural
anthropology of the group. But insofar as ethnographic des-
scription was concerned, the wish that was father to the
thought was that we were able to learn about almost all aspects of their culture (7). Under such pressure, we were
tempted to rush along; we settled for verbal description instead of crosschecking with direct observation. We did not
devote sufficient attention to gathering instances of variation (8).

Thus anthropologists concluded that the cultures they
studied tended to be simple. We pointed to the frequency of
uncomplicated technology and tacitly implied that simple

technology correlated with simplicity in other aspects of life and even with simple mentality. We were willing to accept the conclusion that other cultures were simpler and more clearcut than ours because such a conclusion reinforced our preconceptions of the "primitives." No wonder we failed to recognize our unmitigated gall in assuming that we could master the totality of someone else's culture in a few short months when they themselves do not accomplish this feat in a whole lifetime.

Simplicity implies homogeneity and to a lesser extent isolation, two other themes unquestioningly accepted by anthropologists. Here, too, the fieldwork situation constituted a drawback for self-correction. I remind you that the distinction between "ideal" and "real" culture -- the first being the general structural configuration used as a set of guidelines around which to pattern living, and the latter being actualization in the form of behavior -- only began to be recognized in the late forties. Other things being equal, normative statements about how things should be done tend to be similar from one informant to another. Furthermore, such delineations of idealized patterns rarely include possible mitigating circumstances or instances of what transpires when two contradictory patterns are called into play simultaneously. Thus, "ideal" culture tends to appear relatively simple compared to "real" behavior.

No matter how difficult it may have been to see that anthropologists had to operate on several analytic levels in describing cultures, I still cannot explain the ease with which we ascribed homogeneity to other cultures unless I invoke cultural bias. At the same time that we were asserting the homogeneity of other cultures, we were using the "key informant" technique (9, 10). This method is predicated on the recognition that some individuals within a culture are more knowledgeable than others in relation to specific topics under investigation. Moreover, we had long recognized the universal existence of the so-called "natural division of labor," by which we meant that duties and responsibilities (and, by extension then, knowledge and expertise) were assigned to members of a society according to age and sex differences. Implicitly, then, we were saying that heterogeneity existed although explicitly we were denying it vehemently. Currently, we are having second thoughts on homogeneity and the amount of participation in one's culture that is possible for one individual (11, 12).

Isolation was a theme reinforced by the difficulty we experienced in arriving at our field destinations: if it was hard for us to get in, it seemed reasonable to suppose that it would be equally difficult for someone else to travel in or out. The inherent snobbishness of this attitude is obvious: if our advanced technology could not cope, it could not be done. But we should have realized that isolation was a myth because there are very few groups we have visited who insist no other hominids exist; the others may not be quite as human, but they are there. We ignored the plethora of other disconfirming leads, such as presence of trade objects, band or village exchange of spouses, extragroup aggressive behavior (feuds, raids, warfare), extragroup cooperative behavior (regional feasts, rituals, trading rings), not to mention the frequency of seasonal relocations, pilgrimage phenomena, etc. We failed to understand the obvious point that contact does not have to be time- or people-intensive to create and maintain an interdependence of groups.

The themes of simplicity, homogeneity, and isolation rode in tandem with our belief that other cultures had a "traditional" orientation, by which we meant they looked toward the past and resisted change. Once again, we scrupulously ignored evidence already in hand, and once again I can explain our behavior most easily by recourse to cultural bias. For instance, American anthropologists particularly were very familiar with such Native American groups as the Navajo and Plains Indians. In both instances we were aware that extensive overhauls of their cultures had occurred within Euroamerican historic time. For the Plains groups, we had an example, further confirmed by archeological evidence, of a conversion from an agricultural subsistence base to a hunting base through the adoption of the horse complex. The acceptance of this innovation virtually revised the entire culture. (Incidentally, this case reverses the cherished postulated sequence of hunting-gathering into agriculture into industrialization, and is little referred to even now by our cultural evolutionists.) The Navajo accepted the horse with similar enthusiasm; they also embraced sheepherding. Archeological investigations showed them to have been quite incorporative in the past: they had come down from northern North America and settled among the Pueblos, from whom they had borrowed extensively. Nevertheless, anthropologists refer to them as a "traditional group."

Those of us who studied the peoples of Asia knew of the Sherpas and the Tibetans. The Sherpas of Nepal adopted the white potato and incorporated it as an integral part of their culture. These Himalayan mountainclimbers also have made outside climbing expeditions an important component of their economic base. The Tibetans actively brought about their own culture change by importing Buddhism and literacy from south Asia.   They, too, are supposed to be "traditional groups."

All these groups had integrated many new elements into their cultures so successfully that anthropologists would have had a difficult time uncovering the changes without the existence of historical and archeological evidence. Why did we not extrapolate worldwide and adopt the working assumption that all cultures are receptive to great changes if such innovations are considered helpful? Why did we not see that the concept of traditionalism is not valid?

The primitive/civilized dichotomy bolstered our belief in evolutionary unidirectional progress. Since we were convinced that civilization was a more recent stage of human development than uncivilized cultures and since we saw ample evidence that many "primitives" were becoming civilized, we were led to two additional conclusions: (1) our kind of culture, with its dependence on ever-increasing technology, was an evolutionary imperative, and (2) having gotten there first, we had more experience with this newer phase and, therefore, should show the rest of the world how to duplicate it, to speed along the inevitable. In other words, what "we" had was better than what "they" had; by extension, "we" knew better than "they" did. We were "modern," and they, "backward." We were "developed," and they, "underdeveloped" or "developing," and they had to catch up. What an enormously ego-enriching milieu in which to live, providing one belongs to the proper side of the contrast pair! But also, what a house of cards these premises are!

Self-correction became feasible with a burgeoning of total anthropological people-hours expended in research. This increase came about in four basic ways. (1) More individuals entering the field allowed us to send several people simultaneously to the same area. Cooperative endeavors, with data sharing, resulted in greater data accumulation and in less of a sense of personal proprietary interest in the group so that it has become unfashionable to refer to the people one has studied as "my" tribe and to dissuade others from studying the same group. (2) Increasing ease of transportation, coupled with outside funding sources, made possible repeated trips to the same group so that data collection even by the same individual could be more thorough. (3) A changing focus within the field increased the number of individuals who chose not to follow the usual standard procedures but to commit themselves to ongoing research among a group for a decade or more. For example, I chose to research <u>Rom</u> Gypsies in New York City, where I also earned my living and raised my family; consequently, I have been

able to follow them in detail for thirty years (13), and still
I am learning from them (14). (4) Still others, like Dina
Dahbani-Miraglia (15), are beginning to pursue extended
field studies among groups to which they themselves belong
and among whom they continue to live.

As the ecological perspective began to pervade anthropology, we reviewed and saw that what we had been calling a
simple way of life was an efficient and delicately balanced
articulation with the physical environment. We began to suspect that the ability to serve as substitute in various activities might better be labelled "versatility" than "homogeneity." Generalists are becoming as respectable as specialists these days in more fields than medicine; indeed,
one begins to hear faint mutterings about the dangers of
over-specialization.

The ecological perspective refers to continuous adjustments among parts, one of the basic tenets of anthropology, but the ecological view introduces the concept of recurrent cycles so that the newer emphasis focusses more
sharply on adjustments and readjustments among ever-changing
parts, these adjustments contingent upon circumstances, also
continually in flux.

The work of the applied anthropologists produced another
set of data undermining our conventional wisdom: the vaunted
superiority of our technology failed to prove out universally. Machinery broke down in no time flat when used in
Central Asia. The introduction of irrigation systems to
increase agricultural productivity resulted in severe soil
deterioration through salination, or induced schistosomi-
asis in the farmers. Lack of time precludes mention of the
extensive data on our reluctant recognition that our technical know-how all too often was technical know-not (16, 17).

These new developments have led to some changes in our
discipline's thinking, but a gradual patching up is no longer satisfactory. We are beginning to apply Band-Aids over
the Band-Aids. What we need now is a new Kuhnian paradigm
(18). I propose that we proceed from a somewhat different
set of postulates and a few caveats, and rethink our mate-
rials from a general assumption of flux -- not "change," but
"changingness." The model with which I work is that of individuals continuously choosing among options throughout
their daily existences. It focusses on decision-making; I
have called it choice-taking (14) only to set it off from
that body of literature that has emphasized decision-making
among those in authority and/or with power. Other anthropologists may well formulate different processual models which

may prove more satisfactory for our future purposes. All I
call for is a basic emphasis on continuously adjusting process.

The basic postulate, that (1) culture is constantly
changing, presupposes one stating that (2) culture is trans-
missible. Coupled with the tenets that (3) the various parts
of culture are interrelated and that (4) the sociocultural
system is interdependent with both the physical environment
and a set of human beings who are both sociocultural and biological entities, we have a sufficient basis for a flux
model. We must also specify that (5) culture is cumulative
in the sense that it is incorporative and that certain cultural inventions require the prior existence of certain
others, but there is a caveat here to which I shall refer
shortly. The acknowledgement that culture is transmitted also carries along the idea that (6) much of it tends to be
replicated from one generation to the next, other things being equal -- provided that we remember that other things
rarely are equal. (Continuity also is facilitated because
of the overlap between human generations.) Next, we need a
postulate to the effect that (7) if a sociocultural system
is in existence at a given moment and if its carriers seem
to be perpetuating themselves both biologically and culturally, then we may assume that the total thrust of the culture is more adaptive than maladaptive for the particular
circumstances that presently prevail. Allow me to point out
that this last postulate assumes neither that every item in
the cultural inventory is adaptive nor that the particular
circumstances of the moment will continue in the near or intermediate future (I am willing to bet that they will alter
in the distant future). I cannot go along with the Panglos-
sian ecological assumption that, merely because something
exists today and shows evidence of having existed for some
duration in the past, it is automatically to be considered
useful. I think it quite possible that a sociocultural system, like a breeding population, can carry a load of deleterious items and still survive. However, I am willing to con-
cede that most cultural items are multifunctional and therefore may well be useful in some respects while neutral or
harmful in others.

Finally, we need to rework our ideas on the comparative
method, one of our basic thinking tools (6, 19, 20). Comparison is no more and no less magical than any other scientific technique. It can be used productively or invidi-
ously. It must be phrased neutrally; that is, the working
definitions of the variables must not only be formulated so
that researchers can agree on the coding but also be
stripped of all latent judgment bias. This, in turn,

presupposes a reevaluation of the written sources used in
such data bases as the Human Relations Area Files. For instance, as an experienced medical anthropologist, I object
strenuously to reliance on literature stating that there is
a single disease causation theory in a culture. Medical anthropologists find that there always are several such causa-
tive explanations (and frequently there are many) (21) -- unless insufficient, short-term research has been conducted.
Thus, the new comparative method would require the production of bias-free schemata (22), and a most circumspect
design of the question(s) being posed. I suspect that, at
the present state of our science, too broad a question in-
vites undetected bias in the investigation.

The working caveats we need all stem from past experience: I propose that we keep them up front and utilize them
as standard checking procedures. (1) The first one warns
that things are rarely as simple or homogeneous as they may
first seem. If anthropologists come across a phenomenon or
a set of sociocultural items that seems simple, they should
recheck to insure they have not missed data along the way.
I would elaborate this to warn that genuine simplicity is
not simple; it is not "across the board," and not necessarily a beginning phase in a sequence. (2) The second
caveat is to beware of dichotomous thinking; it may be a
figment of one's cultural conditioning. If an analysis
seems to indicate duality of structure, one should try a bit
harder to see if there is not something else involved. Even
"living vs. dead" is an artificial, Euroamerican duality; we
are beginning to see this as we deal with the issue of when
a person should be declared dead and hence removed from life
support systems to furnish donor organs for others. (3)
Next, any sort of analysis leading us to a conclusion that
reinforces our cultural predilections must be regarded as
highly suspect. Technology may be able to move objects, but
it is not necessarily the prime mover in terms of cause-and-
effect. We Euroamericans have manipulated technology and
brought about changes; others have manipulated social and
ideological variables and effected alterations. Moreover,
technical know-how is not monolithic; that is, it is not all
bunched together as the exclusive possession of Euroamerican
science nor is ours the only form thereof. When we say, "It
can't be done," what we really mean is that we do not know
how to do it. It does not necessarily follow that others
lack knowledge of how to proceed. Or, we may say that it
cannot be done any other way than ours; again, this is more
an admission of our ignorance than a statement of reality
for all cultures (24). A further corollary is that technological expertise is not necessarily superior to social or

political know-how; it is just different. What I am saying
is that all the variables are dependent and all are constantly shifting. If we choose to intervene, we can select any
one of a number of different entrypoints and accelerate
change throughout the system. Thus, many options are open
to us.

Finally, and very importantly, (4) as soon as we find
ourselves thinking linearly, a symptom of which is the desire to use the word, "inevitable," we should stop short and
reexamine with extreme care. There are too many variables
in flux to endorse the concept of inevitability. Moreover,
although I accept the idea of partial determinism, I am not
prepared to advocate a concept of total determinism of any
sort. I work with the assumption that choice abounds. If
you like, this is a Mertonian self-fulfilling hypothesis.
But so is the converse: if we pronounce the verdict of "inevitable" and thus stop trying, we have made it inevitable
through our surrender. On the other hand, if we bring in
the verdict of "not necessarily," we give ourselves intellectual time and space in which to maneuver, searching for
solutions to problems by putting our knowledge together with
that of the rest of the world. Lack of inevitability also
carries along the injunction to keep monitoring this world
of ours, to be aware that (5) there are no final solutions
to anything. Here again, this means that we must work co-
operatively throughout the world, all giving and all taking
from a shared pool of knowledge. Lack of inevitability further means that we do not have to do something even if we
possess the wherewithal for the doing. The Mayans and Tibetans well understood the principle of the wheel but chose
not to capitalize on it for transportation. The Chinese
had the potential for gunpowder but chose fireworks instead.
We do not have to utilize energy-consuming technology if we
do not want to. And, emphatically, we do not have to put
into practice our knowledge of warfare.

Ruth Benedict warned years ago that we will not have a
picture in depth of humankind until members of every culture
have a chance to report on all cultures. A. L. Kroeber put
it somewhat differently when he argued that the intellectual
peaks of any human culture occur when that culture is
in contact with, and receptive to, many other cultures (23).
Thus, much as I have argued for a rethinking of our discipline, I have gone full cycle, for my message is similar to
theirs in urging all of us to phase provincialism out of our
work and to encourage a speedier incorporation of non-Euro-
american inputs into our conceptualizations, theories, and
practice.

References and Notes

1. F.L.K. Hsu, Am. Anth., 75, 1 (1973).
2. C.M. Arensberg and A.H. Niehoff, Introducing Social Change (Aldine-Atherton, Chicago, 1971), 2nd. ed., pp. 21-31.
3. E.T. Hall, The Silent Language (Fawcett Publications, Inc., Greenwich, Conn., 1961), pp. 19-21.
4. A. Kohn, Perspectives in Bio. and Med., 21, 420 (1978).
5. C. Laderman, Conceptions and Preconceptions: Childbirth and Nutrition in Rural Malaysia, Ph.D. thesis, Columbia Univ., Dept. of Anthro. (forthcoming).
6. D.G. Mandelbaum, in Anthropology for the Future, D. Shimkin, S. Tax and J.W. Morrison, Eds. (Dept. of Anthro., Univ. of Illinois, Urbana, 1978), pp. 25-26.
7. This conviction now is being questioned. See (6) and Mead's statement reported by S. Katz in Shimkin, Tax and Morrison, op. cit., p. 241.
8. B.B. Miller and R.J. Miller, in Shimkin, Tax and Morrison, op. cit., p. 104.
9. T.R. Williams, Field Methods in the Study of Culture (Holt, Rinehart and Winston, New York, 1967), pp. 28-31.
10. P.J. Pelto and G.H. Pelto, Anthropological Research (Cambridge Univ. Press, Cambridge, 1970), 2nd. ed., pp. 71-75.
11. R. Wessing in Shimkin, Tax and Morrison, op. cit., p. 171.
12. S. Tax in Shimkin, Tax and Morrison, op. cit., p. 1.
13. R.C. Gropper, Trans. of the N.Y. Acad. of Sci., ser. II, 29, 1050 (1967).
14. R.C. Gropper, Gypsies in the City (The Darwin Press, Princeton, 1975).
15. D. Dahbani-Miraglia, "Both Fish and Fowl: The Insider as Outsider," Ms. (1979).
16. M.T. Farvar and J.P. Milton, Eds., The Careless Technology (The Natural History Press, Garden City, 1972).
17. R.J. Congden, Ed., Introduction to Appropriate Technology (Rodale Press, Emmaus, 1977).
18. T. Kuhn, The Structure of Scientific Revolutions, in O. Neurath, R. Carnap and C. Morris, Eds., Foundations of the Unity of Science (Chicago, The University of Chicago Press, 1970), 2nd. ed., enl., pp. 54-272.
19. H.I. Safa in Shimkin, Tax and Morrison, op. cit., pp. 255, 258.
20. F.K. Lehman in Shimkin, Tax and Morrison, op. cit., p. 260.
21. See, for example, some of the articles in J.B. Loudon, Ed., Social Anthropology and Medicine (London, Academic Press, 1976).

22. I have attempted this for ethnomedicine: R.C. Gropper, Toward a Universal Comparative Medicine, mimeo., 1967.
23. A.L. Kroeber, Configurations of Culture Growth (Univ. of California Press, Berkeley, 1944).
24. R.I. Ford in Material Culture, H. Lechtman and R. Merrill, Eds. (West Publishing Company, St. Paul, 1977), pp. 139-154.

Bibliography

Arensberg, Conrad M., and Arthur H. Niehoff. 1971. Introducing Social Change. 2nd. ed. Chicago and New York. Aldine-Atherton.

Congden, R. J. (ed.). 1977. Introduction to Appropriate Technology: Toward a Simpler Life-Style. Emmaus, Pa. Rodale Press.

Dahbani, Miraglia, Dina. 1979. "Both Fish and Fowl: The Insider as Outsider." Ms.

Farvar, M. Taghi, and John P. Milton (ed.). 1972. The Careless Technology: Ecology and International Development. Garden City, N.Y. The Natural History Press.

Ford, Richard I. 1977. "The Technology of Irrigation in a New Mexico Pueblo." In Heather Lechtman and Robert Merrill (ed.): Material Culture: Styles, Organization, and Dynamics of Technology. 1975 Proceedings of the American Ethnological Society. St. Paul, etc. West Publishing Company. Pp. 139-54.

Hall, Edward T. 1961 reissue of 1959 ed. The Silent Language. A Premier Book. Greenwich, Conn. Fawcett Publications, Inc.

Gropper, Rena C. 1975. Gypsies in the City: Culture Patterns and Survival. Princeton, N.J. The Darwin Press.

————. 1967[a]. Toward a Universal Comparative Medicine. A Working Paper prepared for the Folk Healthways Newsletter. mimeo.

————. 1967[b]. "Urban Nomads -- The Gypsies of New York City." Transactions of the New York Academy of Sciences. ser. II. 29: 1050-56.

Hsu, Francis L. K. 1973. "Prejudice and Its Intellectual Effect in American Anthropology." American Anthropologist. 75: 1-19.

Katz, Solomon. 1978. "The Bio-Social Interface, An Overview." In Demitri Shimkin, Sol Tax and John W. Morrison (ed.): Anthropology for the Future. Research Report No. 4. Urbana, Ill. Department of Anthropology,
University of Illinois. Pp. 240-48.

Kohn, Alexander. 1978. "Errors, Fallacies, or Deception?"
Perspectives in Biology and Medicine. 21: 420-30.

Kroeber, Alfred Louis. 1944. Configurations of Culture
Growth. Berkeley. University of California Press.

Kuhn, Thomas. 1970. "The Structure of Scientific Revolutions." In Otto Neurath, Rudolf Carnap and Charles
Morris (ed.): Foundations of the Unity of Science. II:
54-272. 2nd. ed., enl. Chicago and London. The University of Chicago Press.

Laderman, Carol. (forthcoming). Conceptions and Preconceptions: Childbirth and Nutrition in Rural Malaysia. Ph.
D. thesis, Department of Anthropology, Columbia University.

Lehman, F. K. 1978. "Symbolic Anthropology and the Psycho-
social Interface: Searches for an Epistemology." In
Demitri Shimkin, Sol Tax and John W. Morrison (ed.):
Anthropology for the Future. Research Report No. 4.
Urbana, Ill. Department of Anthropology, University of
Illinois. Pp. 259-65.

Loudon, J. B. (ed.). 1976. Social Anthropology and Medicine. A.S.A. Monograph 13. London. Academic Press.

Mandelbaum, David G. 1978. "The Potentials of Anthropology." In Demitri Shimkin, Sol Tax and John W. Morrison
(ed.): Anthropology for the Future. Research Report
No. 4. Urbana, Ill. Department of Anthropology, University of Illinois. Pp. 24-41.

Miller, Beatrice B., and Robert J. Miller. 1978. "People
as Biocultural Systems: Concepts and Analytic Approaches for the Anthropology of the Future." In Demitri
Shimkin, Sol Tax and John W. Morrison (ed.): Anthropology for the Future. Research Report No. 4. Urbana,
Ill. Department of Anthropology, University of Illinois. Pp. 101-10.

Pelto, Pertti J., and Gretel H. Pelto. 1978. Anthropological Research: The Structure of Inquiry. 2nd. ed. Cambridge, etc. Cambridge University Press.

Safa, Helen I. 1978. "Human Ecology--Models for Human
    Survival: A Review of Development Anthropology Today."
    In Demitri Shimkin, Sol Tax and John W. Morrison
    (ed.): Anthropology for the Future. Research Report No.
    4. Urbana, Ill. Department of Anthropology, University
    of Illinois. Pp. 254-58.

Tax, Sol. 1978. "Toward an Open Scholarly Society for
    World Anthropology." In Demitri Shimkin, Sol Tax and
    John W. Morrison (ed.): Anthropology for the Future.
    Research Report No. 4. Urbana, Ill. Department of
    Anthropology, University of Illinois. Pp. 1-8.

Wessing, Robert. 1978. "The Place of Symbols in Human In-
    teraction." In Demitri Shimkin, Sol Tax and John W.
    Morrison (ed.): Anthropology for the Future. Research
    Report No. 4. Urbana, Ill. Department of Anthropology,
    University of Illinois. Pp. 171-80.

Williams, Thomas Rhys. 1967. Field Methods in the Study of
    Culture. Studies in Anthropological Methods. New
    York, etc. Holt, Rinehart and Winston.

3. Plutocratic Perspectives on Class and Intelligence in America

Anthropologists, other social scientists, and other scientists are not born into ivory towers. Like everyone else, each scientist is born as a baby into a specific society. Like everyone else, prospective scientists are enculturated into the ethnocentric assumptions and common folk notions prevalent in their group. Therefore, we should not be surprised to find that when these individuals become scientists, they sometimes offer, as newly-discovered universal scientific theories, some of the folklore of their own culture.

This being the case, it is the role of a critical scientist to point out the congruence between these allegedly-new scientific theories and well-established folk beliefs -- to show, for example, that biological Creationism is an extension of Christian theology or that Freudian psychology has deep roots in medieval beliefs about witchcraft and sorcery. The implication I am making, of course, is that scientific models which are derived from folk culture should be regarded with particular suspicion. One might even suggest, in the values-laden social sciences, that scholarly ideas which are heretical and outrageous, by folk standards, are more likely to be scientifically and empirically correct than ideas which are readily accepted by lay people.

The purpose of this essay is to show the congruence within American culture among 1) certain folk models of human society; 2) certain recurring scholarly ideas in the social sciences; and 3) certain aspects of American popular culture. Specifically, I wish to show that the central propositions of what T. W. Arnold has called "the folklore of capitalism" find at least two significant reflections in American culture -- first in the form of recurrent cycles of anthropological racism and classism, such as Social Darwinism, the eugenics movement and sociobiology, and second in American leisure activities such as football, the activities of Junior Achievement and the Boy Scouts. To tie these disparate aspects of culture together, I wish to suggest that it is these play and leisure activities which socialize young Americans, especially including young scientists, so that these scientists later produce social-scientific models which are congruent with the dominant capitalist cosmology.

If this essay is part of any academic tradition, it is probably derived from my late professor of anthropology at Washington University, Jules Henry. It was he who first encouraged me, by his writing, seminars, and personal conversations, to take such a holistic perspective on a complex society. His book, Culture Against Man, is a good example of what I am trying to do here. I also share with Professor Henry some appreciation of the methodological problems involved in making sweeping assertions about the American case. In approaching my own set of problems, for example, I would optimally like to have masses of data which would show, for example, that both Edward Wilson and Irven DeVore were Junior Achievers, that Henry Ford and George Dorsey played monopoly together every afternoon, or that William Graham Sumner and Amos Alonzo Stagg were fraternity brothers. Although I have some of that kind of data, I will be content here merely to show the parallels and similarities -- what Morris Opler has called "themes" and which I call the "congruencies" which exist among the widely divergent aspects of American culture I have chosen to consider (Opler 1945).

The general ideas I wish to trace have to do with perceptions of how American society is stratified. I wish to know which social classes have been described in American folklore, and what significant differences have been perceived to exist among them. In particular, I am interested in the idea that people who are "higher" in socio-economic status are also "better" in their biological and mental attributes. After exploring some of these folk notions concerning qualitative and quantitative differences among social classes, I will then examine how these views are projected into the academic arena, particularly in anthropology, and how these folk values also become part of the leisure time activities I have mentioned.

In adopting a theoretical perspective on my subject, I should acknowledge the contributions of Karl Mannheim and Max Weber to the study of ideology. It was Mannheim who developed what has become the fundamental principle of the scientific analysis of ideology -- the principle that ideas have, as he puts it, a "social locus" (Mannheim 1956:106-110). That is, in a stratified or "class" society such as ours, particular values, cosmologies, ontologies and even -- to use Mannheim's best example, notions of Utopia -- are found more frequently in some social classes than in others. Sometimes, a particular idea is found only within one social class. It is the social scientist's job, therefore, to determine the relationships between a social class's intellectual ideas about the world, and the self interest of that particular class.

As I have mentioned, the idea which concerns us here is the notion of class superiority. Max Weber has told us that, in Europe and America, this idea is the product of the Protestant reformation and the concomitant creation of capitalism. Early Protestant capitalists, during their struggle to become an upper class, described themselves as the "elect" of God, their earthly wealth being the natural result of their spiritual superiority (Weber 1930:131, 179-80). Like other ethnic groups and social classes, the Protestant elite created psychological, social and biological theories which legitimated their pre-eminence in the secular world.

Although Weber has discussed the role of Benjamin Franklin and other Americans in helping to create capitalist ideology (Weber 1930: Ch. 2), it is Digby Baltzell who has described in greater detail the specific intellectual origins of the American industrial upper class. He considers that the period after the Civil War was formative for the group he characterizes as an aristocratic caste. He credits Herbert Spencer with inspiring the ideology which came to be shared by members of this new American upper class. Baltzell says that "the dominant class ideology in America was to be found in the sociology of Herbert Spencer" whose books sold almost four hundred thousand copies in the last three decades of the nineteenth century (Baltzell 1964:99). One salient event in this period was when the British sociologist actually addressed a meeting of the American "great and powerful" at Delmonico's restaurant in New York in 1882 (Baltzell 1964:27).

By mentioning here the important role of Herbert Spencer in creating an American upper class ideology, it might be argued that I am undercutting my assertion that "folk notions" of social structure are historically the most important. So it might be wise to include here a few comments about the relationships between intellectuals and others in a society, as anthropologists have seen such matters.

First we should note, as Paul Radin has done, that all societies maintain an "intellectual class" which creates ideas and makes them available within a society (1957). That is, all societies include a relatively small number of people who actively generate new ideas, or recover old ones, and try to incorporate these ideas into the cultural system. Radin observed this process among the Winnebago Indians and I have seen it myself in fieldwork among the Potawatomis, Cheyennes, and Cherokees. But all of the ideas which are generated and dispersed within a society, as Robertson Smith has noted, do not necessarily become part of the collective folk tradition (1882). Rather, the ideas presented by tribal prophets and native intellectuals which are <u>disfunctional</u> to society tend to be ignored, while ideas which <u>do</u> have a popular interest are seized upon and often elaborated by others.

So when we approach Herbert Spencer from this anthropological perspective, we see him in the role of intellectual for the nascent American corporate aristocracy. He had the same role for them as Crashing Thunder had for the Winnebagoes, Hoseah for the Biblical Hebrews, Handsome Lake for the Senecas, or Sweet Medicine for the Cheyennes. And it is important to note that as students of folk culture, we are much less interested in what Herbert Spencer actually said and wrote than in what he was <u>understood</u> to have said -- what was accepted and preserved in the folk tradition. That is, we are interested in what cosmology was generated in the minds of the "great and powerful" that day in 1882 at Delmonico's, when they sat listening to Herbert Spencer's views on sociology.

In seeking to answer this question, I will once again adopt the posture of an anthropologist. Like any good fieldworker, I will try to find a knowledgeable native informant who can tell me about his perception of reality. Fortunately, in looking for an informant among the American upper class, we have the advantage of dealing with a <u>literate</u> group of people, who have written and published autobiographies, personal impressions, advice, and sometimes polemics and diatribes of various sorts, from Benjamin Franklin to J. Paul Getty.

Spencer and Carnegie

For this formative period of American upper class life, 1860-1890, there are many examples of vocal and articulate ideologues who were themselves members of the emerging upper class but who were not scholars. Prominent among them are Andrew Carnegie, John D. Rockefeller II, and Henry Ford. Of these, I will first consider the most popular writer, Andrew Carnegie, who wrote with considerable color and verve, and whose books sold nearly as well as Spencer's.

I suppose the general outline of Carnegie's life is well known -- he was a poor British immigrant who made a fortune in the steel industry. What we are interested in, however, is not how he made his fortune but how Andrew Carnegie perceived the structure of American society, having risen to the top of it. Carnegie continually quotes and mentions Spencer in his several books, so we might ask, How did Carnegie understand the model of industrial society offered by Spencer?

Carnegie's best representation of his sociological views is his book <u>Triumphant Democracy</u>, published in 1893. His Chapter 2, entitled "The American People," begins with the following quote from Spencer (Carnegie 1893:24): "From biological truths it may be inferred that the eventual mixture of the allied varieties of the Aryan race forming the population, will produce a finer type of man than has hitherto existed." Carnegie himself unabashedly speaks of an Anglo-American "master race" (1893:24). The last part of his book is a plea for political unity between Britain and America. A few direct quotes from Carnegie will give us the general flavor of his social views. Then I will present a diagram representing Carnegie's model of caste and class in American society.

> These little islands in the North Sea, which rule one-sixth of the whole world and one-fifth of its people, draw mastery not from natural advantages, but from the "happy breed of men" which inhabit them. These islanders have been the conquering race. In the struggle for existence they have proved themselves the fittest... A good lineage this for any people, and fortunately for the Americans they are essentially British (Carnegie 1893:24-25).

> Thus the American of to-day is certainly more than three-fourths British in his ancestry. The other fourth is principally German; for more than four and a half millions of these educated, thrifty, and law-abiding citizens were received between 1840 and 1890, more even than from Ireland. Hence the American, three parts British, one part German, is almost as purely Anglo-Saxon as either Briton or German. These three nations are really one people. From all countries other than Britain and Germany, the immigration during the past fifty years was little more than five millions. . . .It may, however, safely be averred that the small mixture of foreign races is a decided advantage to the new race, for even the British race is improved by a slight cross (Carnegie 1893:26-27).

In creating his model of American society, Carnegie drew heavily on the U.S. Census of 1890. He worked with a figure of 61 million for total population, of which he counted 55 million as white, and 6 million as Negro. In constructing a diagram of Carnegie's cosmology of America (Figure 1), I have tried to preserve these statistical proportions as areas of the population pyramid.

It can be seen from Carnegie's model that he considered class and caste to be largely coterminous in American society. Capitalists and their managers could only be drawn from Anglo-American stock, while non-Aryan but white Americans could only hope, at best, to become skilled workers (1893:129). Negroes were

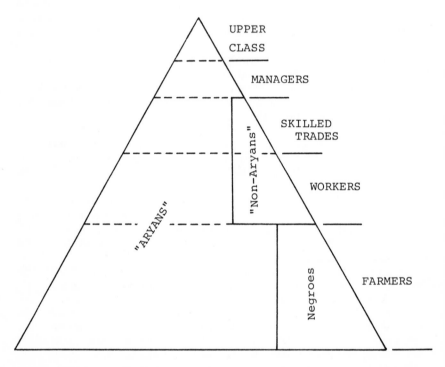

Figure 1. Andrew Carnegie's Cosmology of America.

rural and agricultural. Carnegie predicted, erroneously, that they would constitute a decreasing proportion of the American population.

Social mobility, then, was mostly a phenomenon among Anglo-Americans, since the other races, or as Carnegie sometimes put it, "the defective classes," could not overcome their inherent disabilities (Carnegie 1893:176). That is, Anglo-Americans competed among themselves to climb up the pyramid from rural or working-class background to the pinnacle of being a wealthy industrialist, like Carnegie. So what were these differences between those who were mobile and those who were not?

Carnegie's list of beneficent traits will be so familiar to Americans that I believe, in the interests of overcoming our ethnocentrism, we should look cross-culturally at traits which are regarded by other societies as likely to result in upward mobility. The most prominent of these around the world is probably lineage or ancestry. Most tribal people are not surprised when a man of distinguished ancestry rises to high places. This common human notion is perceived in the English slogan, "blood will tell." Another trait frequently rewarded is large size. Tall, muscular, or even exceptionally corpulent men frequently bear the burden of high expectations from their tribal fellows. Luck is another trait which many tribal peoples look for in their leaders -- a demonstrated history of being lucky. This reached an institutionalized status among Viking adventurers, prominent among whom is "Leif the Lucky."

But these measurable and ascertainable traits are not the ones which Carnegie says are important for success in industrial society. Instead, his virtues are abstract and hark back to early capitalism and the virtues upheld by "Poor Richard" (Franklin 1928). In his book the Empire of Business Carnegie catalogued and discussed those particular traits which he felt resulted in high achievement among industrial managers, and which he was prepared to reward among his employees. First among these was genius, mentioned long and frequently. Other traits include ability, concentration, honesty, energy, judgment, philanthropy, frugality, sobriety, and perhaps surprisingly, being open-minded and without prejudice (1902:111, 113, 121, 122, 192, 200, 205). Scientifically, these concepts are at about the same level as popular astrology, since nearly everyone can be described as having the traits to some degree, or not having them, for that matter. That is, if an industrial manager wished to promote his son-in-law, it would be easy to manipulate the categories so that the son-in-law seemed eminently superior in character to other candidates for promotion. The categories then serve as a mask for implementing whatever prejudices one would care to exercise -- nepotism, racism or classism.

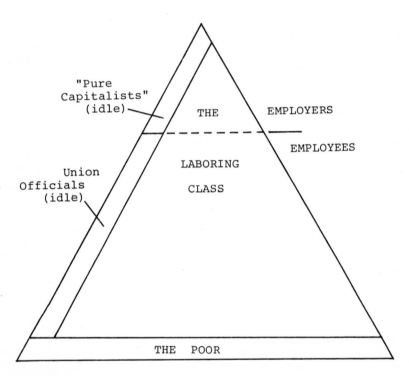

Figure 2.   Henry Ford's Cosmology of America.

The Ford Amendments

Like Carnegie, Henry Ford was an intellectual member of the aristocracy who write popular books and had some influence on American culture. Like Carnegie, Ford envisioned a cosmology or sociology of American society, of which the most remembered feature is probably his adamant anti-Semitism (Ford 1923:250-52). But Ford differed from Carnegie in admitting many "non-Aryan" persons into his conception of social mobility. In fact, he projected his model of an industrial corporation onto his model of America, but with little regard for the kind of census data which Carnegie considered to be important. If we can create a schematic diagram from Chapter 18 of his autobiography, it would like Figure 2.

One interesting feature of Ford's cosmology is how little he mentions race or ethnicity, except for "the Jewish Question." This attitude toward the relative unimportance of ethnicity (at least among non-Jewish whites) is also reflected in the enrollment policies of several educational institutions he founded -- the Henry Ford Trade School (Ford 1926:180-185), the Edison Institute of Technology, and the Greenfield Village (Ford 1930:268-279).

Ford's cosmological removal of ethnic barriers among whites reflects, of course, the importance of Mediterranean and East European workers in the Ford plants. Unlike Carnegie, Ford employed several hundred thousand white "ethnics" in his plants, and he was fond of noting such things as "The Polish workmen seem to be the cleverest of all the foreigners" (1923:100). Ford was, then, apparently sensitive to the potential for labor trouble along ethnic lines. One way of reading his philosophy and educational programs is to see them as holding out the hope of social mobility for white immigrant workers. Ford's list of traits which result in social mobility among whites is very similar to Carnegie's. He lists genius, invention, self-reliance, cooperation, fidelity and athletic ability (Ford 1930:267, 270-9; 1926:177-185).

Ford's exclusion of Negroes from his cosmology also deserves to be mentioned, and to be put within an historical perspective. Although black workers have come to dominate the auto industry in Detroit (Georgakas and Surkin 1975), these developments were after Ford's active period as a writer. Ford mostly ignored Negroes in his cosmology, and he did not predict that they would later be actively recruited from southern farms to undercut the militant union organizations of white workers in Ford factories (Boyer and Morais 1955:231-266). Like Carnegie, Ford grossly underestimated the political significance which Negro people would come to have.

In describing the cosmologies of Carnegie and Ford, and also of Franklin Roosevelt, to follow, I should emphasize that I am not interested so much in their success in implementing the cosmologies they described. Nor am I particularly interested in how accurate they were, scientifically, in describing American class structure. But I am extremely interested in the structure of these cosmologies, the circumstances of their invention, their ideological functions, and how they were projected into other aspects of American culture -- scholarship and games. In fact, it is amazing to note the extent to which folk cosmologies are immune to scientific criticism. When folk beliefs are revised, it is usually not because of the logic employed by scientific scholars in attacking them, but because of political pressures or changed socio-economic circumstances, such as, in the case of Ford, labor scarcity and the immigration of European workers.

An extreme example of ideological resistance to scientific criticism is provided by the Ku Klux Klan in the United States and its public arm, the National States Rights Party of Savannah, Georgia. Through the publication of its newspaper, The Thunderbolt, the NSRP continues to promote the sale of racist classics such as Professor Charles Carroll's The Negro--A Beast or in the Image of God (Carroll 1968). Among The Thunderbolt's most bizarre anthropological theories is that native Africans were originally the offspring of Hamite refugees from the Near East and African great apes! Apparently no amount of evidence from genetics or paleoanthropology is sufficient to convince the several thousand readers of The Thunderbolt that such an event could not (biologically) and did not (historically) occur. As long as such beliefs have a political and social utility, they seem to remain as a foundation for the shared folk cosmology of a particular group.

New Deal Cosmology

In the 1930 s, there were political and economic events which caused yet another revision in the cosmology maintained by American aristocrats, and a bifurcation of cosmological positions. It was the Great Depression which caused a split to appear, ideologically, between those who upheld the old ideology and became known as conservatives, and the New Deal Democrats under Franklin Roosevelt, who took the mantle of Liberalism.

In this historical period, the prominent ideological protagonists were no longer the aristocrats themselves, but rather their middle-class hired help, in a tendency toward technocracy already decried by Henry Ford in 1923. Both liberal and conservative political figures, he said, encouraged the careers of "a class of writers who are writing what they think will please their employers" (Ford 1923:254).

In defense of the old cosmology were such writers as Cromwell and Czerwosky (1937), Snyder (1940) and Withers (1920). On the attack were the proponents of the new order, Hopkins (1963), Arnold (1942) and Roosevelt himself.

In reading Roosevelt's own words, we discover that he is not nearly as elegant an informant as Carnegie or Ford (Roosevelt 1934). He was, on the one hand, very abstruse in his political speeches and very specific in his personal memoranda. Fortunately, however, Bernard Asbell has synthesized Roosevelt's general views on American society after reading a great portion of the original material (Asbell 1973). In reading Asbell, one cosmological contrast we can see immediately between Roosevelt and Ford-Carnegie, is that Roosevelt presents not one but two pictures of American society. Roosevelt describes on the one hand how he thinks American society is, and then suggests what it should be. With Ford and Carnegie, however, the proponents of the status quo, we see that how things are and how they should be are one and the same.

It is difficult to present Roosevelt's picture of the realities of American society graphically, because he saw it in at least three dimensions. As two cross-cutting parameters of the way things are, he saw continua from rich to poor and from rural to urban. Complicating his sociological picture were ethnic and religious divisions, some coterminous with stratification and urbanism, others not. After describing the major social parameters of the American electorate -- rich-poor, North-South, Protestant-Catholic-Jew -- Asbell adds, speaking for Roosevelt (1973:79): "And all these groupings divide and subdivide: rural and urban, artisans and shopkeepers, immigrants and native Americans, union workers and non-union workers, employed and unemployed".

One way of understanding Roosevelt's picture of the status quo is to consider him primarily as a politician counting votes. He was putting together a "majority of minorities" and he wanted to emphasize those sociological variables which influenced voting behavior. Unlike Carnegie and Ford, Roosevelt did not stress the mental or behavioral qualities which were supposed to characterize the different sections of American society, but rather the political issues which separated them. By omission, the implication is that genetic or "natural" differences among races and ethnic groups are not very important.

This impetus for full equality among races and ethnic groups and between the sexes is continued in the liberal wing of the Democratic Party to this day, and has become increasingly more explicit. In place of Eleanor Roosevelt's mostly symbolic endorsements of Negro causes (1961), there are Equal Opportunity laws and federal scrutiny of what proportions of "minorities" are represented in federal agencies and institutions receiving federal funds. The same Utopian model of American society is represented in Roosevelt's speeches and in the activities of liberal Democrats

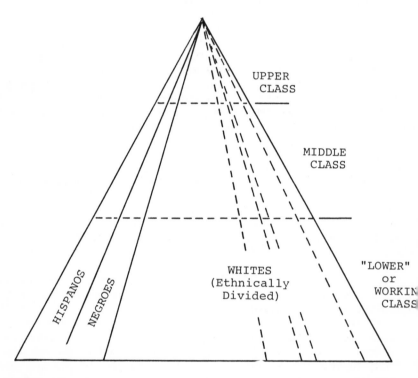

Figure 3.   The New Deal's Cosmology of America.

until modern times. As Roosevelt put it repeatedly, he did not wish
to challenge the structure of American capitalist society, but only
to ensure that all Americans had "equal opportunity" to become
members of all strata.

Since the New Deal, government planners have used a three-
level model of American society, adding a "middle" class. If we
project on that model the Utopian expectations of liberal
Democrats, we get the cosmology of Figure 3.

Although Figure 3 represents the dominant shared cosmology
among those creating and implementing federal programs, it is not
the only cosmology presently advocated by influential people (Turner
and Starnes 1976). The older cosmology of the aristocracy is still
around, although in somewhat subdued form. As with the New Deal
cosmology, the older cosmology is now advocated mostly by middle-
class writers, with the notable exception of J. Paul Getty, whose
writings have been popularized by Playboy magazine (Getty 1971).
Perhaps the best known advocate of the old cosmology has been Ayn
Rand, whose active career as a writer began with the publication in
1936 of We the Living. Through her novels, a play, a journal -- The
Objectivist -- and clubs and study groups, she has promoted her
particular philosophical views with great success. Her students and
proteges include several important political figures, for example
Alan Greenspan (Greenspan 1967).

Like the New Dealers, Rand too has a Utopian model of
American society. In her view, most societal problems could be
solved by the removal of government and other restrictions on "free
enterprise," thereby allowing the cream of society to rise to the top.
She is not heavily sociological in her viewpoint, however, like
Carnegie, or even as much as Ford, but rather takes a psychological
perspective. She is convinced, like Carnegie, Ford, and Ben
Franklin, that free enterprise results in the social mobility upwards
of people possessing certain beneficent psychological
characteristics. From among these characteristics, she emphasizes
the importance, like Getty (1971:93), of the ability to innovate, or
"genius." As a moral philosopher, Rand argues that if people of
genius are allowed to pursue their own self-interest, then society as
a whole benefits (1967). In her book, The Virtue of Selfishness
(1964), she argues for the encouragement of selfishness in society
and the discouragement of its "evil" opposite -- altruism.

Like all her cosmological predecessors back to Ben Franklin,
Rand argues for the scientific reality of certain moral or psychic
categories which are extremely abstract. But from an anthropological perspective, we should point out that these categories are also
very arbitrary and ethnocentric. That is, they are very American
and not very scientific.

As anthropologists, we note for example that people around the world divide up the color spectrum and name the colors very differently (Conklin 1955). Similarly, different societies divide up the moral spectrum very differently. That is, just as linguistic color categories in English (red, yellow, blue) are entirely cultural and have no scientific significance, neither do English moral categories (selfish, altruistic, cooperative, innovative, etc.). For a comparative example of moral notions, let me discuss the idea of Xama among traditional Cheyenne Indians.

If you were to ask a Cheyenne elder what kinds of traits would result in health, long life, and happiness for an individual, you would probably be told that it is most important to be Xama—to be part of the natural order of the universe. This order is ensured ritually by the tribal Sun Dance, and personally by one's prayers, fasting, and religious quests. Xama-individuals are at peace with God and other people, and especially with birds and animals. By being in this state, they avoid illness and natural disasters. They avoid alcohol, hold jobs, and have a comfortable family life.

If the Cheyenne people ever develop a university where clinical psychology is practiced, it seems likely to me that one of the first problems which will interest them is Xama. No doubt Cheyenne psychologists will try to invent test situations which will demonstrate whether or how much Xama a test subject might have. A scale of 100 might be devised with happy, healthy, and unscarred nonegenarians at the top and perhaps accident-prone, lightning-struck, epileptic teen-agers at the bottom.

While it might seem peculiar to imagine a Cheyenne psychologist embarked on such an enterprise, we shall see that beginning about 1850, European and American scholars began a similar ethnocentric quest. But instead of Xama, they were looking for Genius, by which they sought to explain why some people were rich and others poor. And if they have consistently failed to operationalize the notion of genius to everyone's satisfaction, they have at least managed to put the quest for genius at the very highest level of prestige in Western scholarship.

Head Shape and Head Content

In the previous sections of this essay, I have described two cosmological views of American society which are not only different in content but different in type. The first, which I derive from Carnegie, rationalizes the status quo and is both sociological and psychological. The second, which I have attributed mostly to Franklin Roosevelt, emphasizes a Utopian model of American society, and constantly criticizes the status quo for not measuring up to ideal standards.

In this part of my essay, I wish to show how the efforts of academic people have supported both cosmological perspectives. However, since so much serious effort has already been devoted to the intellectual history of this period (Hofstadter 1944, Montagu et. al. 1975), I wish to set some manageable limits to my inquiry. Here I will only discuss episodes of academic debate in which anthropologists were enlisted to defend the cosmological views I have described. I will discuss the cosmological and political implications of the work of George Dorsey, Franz Boas, Clark Wissler, Bernhard Stern, Robert Briffault, Ashley Montagu, Lionel Tiger, Robin Fox, and Marshall Sahlins.

The first episode I will consider, the debate on "race" between Franz Boas and other anthropologists, must be understood within a context of intense institutional competition. When Boas sought to establish anthropology as a university discipline in the United States, beginning about the turn of the century, he was immediately brought into conflict with the "native" anthropology, which was based in museums and in a government agency, the Bureau of American Ethnology (Stocking 1968:284-296; Moore 1974). These scholars were collectively known as "The Washington School," and for years Boas and his students struggled with the older establishment for money, for control of journals, and for institutional positions. One state of this struggle included the chauvinist and anti-Semitic attacks made against Boas because of his pro-German sentiments in World War I (Stocking 1968:273-5; Moore 1972).

For good reasons, then, Boas' political sympathies were with U.S. immigrant groups in general and with the aristocratic German-Jewish community of New York in particular (Birmingham 1968). It is not surprising to find that a great part of Boas' scholarship was devoted to destroying what he regarded as the myths of inherent ethnic inferiority of immigrants. But Boas' tactic was an interesting one, considering subsequent clashes among intellectuals.

Boas began his studies very modestly, measuring the head shapes of European immigrants and their American-born children. His conclusion was that American-born children were significantly different both from their parents and from foreign-born siblings, showing that the body forms of immigrant groups were not immutable, but had changed significantly in response to the American environment (Boas 1912).

Boas, then, inaugurated the convention in American anthropology of measuring the measurable -- heads, heights, mass, etc. -- and using these traits as analogous or co-variant with those traits which were difficult or impossible to measure -- intelligence and "character." Too, Boas was not reluctant to draw the most profound kinds of political and moral inferences from his measurements of apparently trivial body traits. In 1931, he concluded from his anthropometric work, "There is no reason to believe that one race is by nature so much more intelligent, endowed with great will power, or emotionally more stable than another" (Boas 1931:13-14). That is, the implication was that if the body form of immigrants could change dramatically, so could their mental traits, so that there was no good reason why immigrants should settle for the socio-economic roles which were thrust upon them immediately upon their arrival in the United States. Ultimately, the argument is <u>for</u> social mobility of immigrants upward and <u>against</u> the immutability of the psychological characteristics and stereotypes which are prominent in Carnegie's cosmology.

This analogy between body form and mental traits was not lost on the other side in this controversy. For very soon there was mobilized in Washington a tremendous project in anthropometry which would result in the publication of <u>Race Crossing in Jamaica</u> (Davenport and Steggerda 1929). The principal investigators for this project were C. B. Davenport and Morris Steggerda; advising them was a panel of experts including Boas' old institutional antagonist Clark Wissler (Stocking 1968:283); and financing the project was none other than the Andrew Carnegie Institution of Washington (Davenport and Steggerda 1929:3-5).

Proponents of immutability had been troubled by results from Army intelligence tests which showed that American Negroes from the North were "more intelligent" than Southern whites (Montagu 1945), and by preliminary data from Jamaica which showed that there, too, Negroes were "smarter" (Shuey 1966). This debate, which included collateral discussions of natural selection and hybrid vigor, harks back to Darwin, who noted ironically that some people who opposed his biological principles in theory practiced them every day in breeding animals (Darwin 1859:Ch. 1). We should add the irony that many aristocrats who extolled the virtues of hybrid hounds also alleged that human "mulattoes" were physically degenerate! (Rodenwalt 1927:415).

So the challenge to Davenport and Steggerda was to preserve the ethnic cosmology of Carnegie et. al. by explaining racial variability in Jamaica by reference to immutable racial traits. They proceeded by measuring black, white and brown Jamaicans all over, (cephalic index, foot index, strabismus) and subjecting them to various psychological tests. Their aristocratic sponsors in the United States were no doubt relieved to hear the conclusion that while blacks could learn simple tasks quickly, they had little capacity for creative thought and also "clearly have sense of rhythm exceptionally well developed" (1929:316).

Of course, when these kinds of conclusions are supported by charts and graphs and put into scholarly jargon, they have a rather convincing appearance. But in their "General Discussion", the authors present their views more simply (1929:458-9). They conclude that "the Black. . .is poor at planning, carries mental pictures poorly, and profits little by experience." In explaining why blacks had scored higher than whites on mental tests, the authors compare blacks to calculating machines. They explain the poor performance of whites by saying "that the more complicated a brain,. . .the less satisfactorily it performs the simple numerical problems. . ." That is, they offer the surprising hypothesis that the reason whites do worse on mental tests is that their brain is better! I suppose that if their brains were better yet, they wouldn't be able to do any math at all!

In retrospect, this anthropometric episode in American anthropology might seem very odd. Here we have serious scholars -- Boas funded by his wealthy immigrant patrons, Davenport by the Carnegie Institution -- running about the world measuring people's heads. On the basis of these measurements, they are willing to make profound sociological statements which have immense political consequences. It is also interesting to note that the tempest was in a teapot, for when American immigrants finally moved toward social equality and social mobility, it was not because of moral suasion. Rather, it was because they rallied their electoral power under the New Deal, and Negro Americans <u>demanded</u> further concessions in the 1960 s. I doubt that any proponent of Carnegie's cosmology had his mind changed by the data and arguments offered by Boas, but when immigrants and Negroes banded together as liberal Democrats, the old aristocrats had to take notice and offer concessions. And as Baltzell has noted, Boas and John Dewey emerged as foremost intellectual leaders of the New Deal (1964:273).

Heads and Potatoes

Other episodes among anthropologists in this period are worth mentioning. For example, we should note the role of George Dorsey as defender of the status quo on the one hand and comrade of Chicago industrialists on the other (Cole 1931:413). In two popular books (1925, 1929) Dorsey defended the structure of American industrial society, and noted that American workers "pursue their vocations as zealously as do the great bankers. . .They have found their life work. . .they are content" (Dorsey 1929:150). Oddly, Dorsey persisted in saying this during a period in American history in which workers were striking, picketing, and occasionally engaging in armed revolt (Boyer and Morris 1955).

On the critical side, there was Robert Briffault, an anthropologist who was also a prolific essayist, for such magazines as <u>The Nation</u>, <u>Saturday</u> <u>Review</u>, and <u>Scribner's</u> <u>Magazine</u> (Briffault 1936). He recognized that intelligence tests were being used to justify an educational system in which workers, particularly "ethnic" workers, were being segregated and given the sort of education which would convince them they were inferior. In response, he argued in The Pacific Weekly (1935:59) "The handicap of proletarian intelligence from lack of educational equipment is chiefly effective in giving rise to an incapacity to throw off those burdens of ruling-class traditional wish fulfillment which are largely intended to inculcate loyalty, submissiveness, and stupidity in the ruled. But once that handicap is overcome by the intensification of class opposition, the intelligence of the proletarian is necessarily more effective in its fundamental and vital judgments than the most cultivated intelligence deflected by class tradition."

Briffault's brand of radical-chic Marxism, however, was not the only kind represented in the American debate on intelligence and social mobility. Soon, because of a remarkable series of political events, Briffault's near-Marxist position would be replaced by the real thing, in the person of Bernhard Stern. And if one might already wonder about the relevance of foot index for social mobility, the question of Russian potato yields might seem even less relevant. But as we shall see, even this question was intimately related, in the minds of academic debaters, to cosmological perceptions of society, and especially to the question of how socialism affected human beings.

The central figure in this debate, of course, was Trofim Lysenko, the Soviet geneticist. In a time when Lamarckian ideas were in full retreat in American biology, Lysenko maintained that potatoes and other crops developed by Soviet botanists did in fact inherit acquired characteristics. As president of the Soviet Academy of Agricultural Sciences in 1948, he advocated an emphasis on the teaching of Lamarckian principles in Soviet universities, at the expense of Mendelian principles (Lysenko 1948).

Lysenko's position in the Soviet academy was buttressed, so he said, by the full approval of the Central Committee of the Communist Party and by "J. V. Stalin personally" (Lysenko 1948:48). From his position of influence, Lysenko caused Soviet geneticists to take a terribly wrong fork in the road, theoretically, although he inaugurated many useful techniques for improving strains of fruits and vegetables for use in Russian climates (Proletariat 1979).

The political significance of Lysenko's biology was well understood within the leadership of the Soviet Union. They wished to demonstrate that all of nature, including tomatoes and potatoes, was as agreeable to change as was "Soviet Man," the made-over citizen of the USSR. That is, they wished to show that vegetables, like people, could totally change themselves in a different environment. For people, the new environment was socialism, and Soviet Man was supposed to be the improved strain who would prosper in socialist Russia. Unlike others of his species who were being buffeted about by the uncontrollable Great Depression in capitalist countries, Soviet Man was supposed to be a rational humanist, in firm control of his environment. For this he needed a rational and predictable science of agronomy, not one ruled by "a medley of fortuitous, isolated phenomena, without any necessary connections and subject to no laws" (Lysenko 1948:59). Soviet theoreticians, then, regarded Mendelian genetics as a reflection of "bourgeois" economics, in which apparently uncontrollable laws of nature served as a mask for the oppression and exploitation of workers by capitalists.

The American Communist Party apparently also saw things this way, and this is where the debate on Lysenko becomes relevant to New Deal cosmology. We are able to trace this relevance now because of several recent books on the history of the Communist Party in this period (Starobin 1972, Jaffe 1975). By now it is clear that at a certain point in its development, in part because of the wartime alliance with the Soviet Union, the New Deal turned to the American Communist Party for support, and the CPUSA, in turn, indicated its willingness to cooperate.

In anthropology, Marxist influence on the New Deal was provided by Bernhard Stern of Columbia University. Under New Deal sponsorship, Stern quickly became a thorn in the side of the old-line opponents of the New Deal, by constantly poking holes in some of the most respected myths of capitalism. Writing for the National Resources Committee, for example, he argued that capitalism did not encourage inventiveness, as it claimed, but rather suppressed it (Stern 1938). He exposed the wartime collusion between "the enemy" and General Electric and other American industries (Stern 1943). And when yet another round of the nurture-nature debate began, it was Stern who responded for the nurture side, in the pages of Science (June 23, 1950).

This time, the central document in the debate was Curt Stern's textbook, Principles of Human Genetics (1949). In it, C. Stern argued that the higher socioeconomic classes were genetically superior in intelligence, and bemoaned the fact that the less intelligent classes were demographically more fertile (C. Stern 1949:514-520). In response, Bernhard Stern pointed out that such assertions clearly laid the groundwork for eugenics programs directed against poor, black, or working people (1949, 1950). Such proposals had already been generated, and were funded, once again, by Carnegie money, this time through the Andrew Carnegie Institution of Genetics at Cold Spring Harbor (Stern 1949:317). Bernhard Stern, however, agreed with H. J. Muller that such proposals were "Hitlerite" or "Fascist" (Muller 1935:ix). So this time, only two years (1948-1950) were required to polarize political positions between progressives and conservatives. By contrast, nearly two decades were required in the more naive period between Franz Boas and C. B. Davenport (1910-1929).

When we understand the history of this controversy over race and intelligence in anthropology, we can see that the issues have changed very little since Boas. Jensen, Shockley, Eysenck, and Herrnstein essentially occupy the positions of Curt Stern, Davenport and Steggerda (Montagu 1975). The liberal anthropological establishment, led by Montagu, Dobzhansky, Brace and Livingstone, is in the same progressive tradition as Bernhard Stern, Briffault and Boas (Brace et. al. 1971).

The political consequences of the two positions are also the same. Since race and class are largely coterminous in American society, arguments for racial inferiority are also arguments for class inferiority. And by the time of Curt Stern, the arguments of the conservatives are couched explicitly in terms of class rather than race. Similarly, the recent responses to Jensen and Herrnstein emphasize class rather than race. They are used almost interchangeably.

The immediate political issue, of course, as Briffault noted long ago, is whether the American educational system will be tailored to the "immutability" of class, or whether schools will encourage social mobility. Allen Otten, columnist for the Wall Street Journal, argues that if Jensen and Herrnstein are correct, then public finances must be restructured to counteract "the traditional liberal stress on education" (Otten 1974). He adds, however, that "some" children in the lower classes might still be socially mobile.

The Savage Corporate Manager

In the last two decades, another element has been added to the debate on class superiority -- the idea that animal groups are sociologically analogous to human groups. Ultimately, this kind of thinking has led us to sociobiology, but the initial thrust was provided by Robert Ardrey in African Genesis (1961). In this and subsequent books (1966, 1970), Ardrey pursued the thesis that plains baboons provided the closest analogues of human behavior. Baboons maintained a hierarchy among males, and males on the whole were larger than and outranked females.

Ardrey's thesis could have been more timely, politically, for he soon ran against the potent feminist movement in American politics. Women anthropologists, in particular, marshalled piles of data to counteract the supporters of Ardrey (Rosaldo and Lamphere 1974, Reiter 1975). They showed that choosing the example of baboons tended to support male prejudices, that choosing patas monkeys or gibbons would give entirely different results, results which confirmed feminist political assertions.

The other aspect of Ardrey's theory, concerning male

hierarchy, had a somewhat different history. And here we can see very clearly the interplay between the scholarly and the folk traditions. Between 1961 and the present, books all across this folk-scholarly spectrum have appeared, but supporting the same basic idea -- that "successful" men are inherently superior to other "unsuccessful" men.

Anthropological scholarship for this position was provided by Robin Fox and Lionel Tiger, supplementing Ardrey's own amateur anthropology. In Men in Groups (Tiger 1969) and The Imperial Animal (Tiger and Fox 1971), they argue for the importance of hunting and other aggressive instincts in human male behavior. They consider "aggression" to be a category of nature and say that "One animal has to strive to outdo another for nest sites, territory, food, water, dominance. . ." (Tiger and Fox 1971:209).

At the beginning of this article, in discussing Carnegie and Herbert Spencer, I emphasized that it was less important to analyze what Spencer actually said than what Carnegie and others understood him to say. In assessing the impact of Ardrey-Tiger-Fox on the thinking of modern corporate aristocrats, we should again take the same tack. Our guide for the analysis is a book by the businessman's intellectual, Antony Jay, entitled Corporation Man (1972).

Jay flatters his scholarly mentors by describing them as the authors of a New Biology, whose major proposition is that "the spring of human action (is) not the controlled logical working of the reason, but the uncontrollable surge of much deeper subconscious or unconscious emotional drives" (Jay 1972:17). Further, in looking at industrial society, he says "Status-seeking emerges not as an unworthy failing of jealous executives, but as an immutable ingredient in man's make-up -- an ingredient he shares with many other species including the jackdaw, the baboon and the domestic hen. The same is true of exploring, and aggressive behavior, and defense of territory, and protection of young: they are deep in our nature because the apes and hominids who lacked these qualities died out, while those who had them survived to become our ancestors" (1972:18).

As his book progresses, Jay begins to describe the personal qualities which result in social mobility, and he names them. And as we see the list, we get a feeling of déjà vu -- we've been here before. These are the same qualities which Carnegie, Ford and their contemporaries alleged were present in the corporate elite. Except now, with Jay, these qualities are immutable, and buttressed by the scholarship of Fox and Tiger, as well as Konrad Lorenz and Desmond Morris.

To anyone familiar with the history traced in this essay the current controversy over sociobiology might well be received with a "Ho-Hum" attitude. It is true that Edward Wilson, this time with termites instead of baboons, has argued that genes controlling behavior are located differentially among human beings (1978). He therefore lays the scientific groundwork for theories of race- and class-based genetic superiority. And it is true that this has aroused a loud response from progressive anthropologists, led this time by Marshall Sahlins (1976), who sees the political implications and seeks to counter them. So what else is new?

It is also true that we continue to have two prominent political factions in the American upper class. The liberals seek to maintain power by offering the carrot to the electorate -- the hope of social mobility and better things to come. The conservatives meanwhile proffer the stick, the promise of corrective institutions for the defective classes -- in the form of schools, prisons, or mental hospitals.   And as long as we have progressive and conservative positions in the body politic, we shall certainly have them in the academic arena as well.

Hut-two, Social Darwinism

I have not discussed the social Darwinists Sumner and Keller very much here simply because a great deal has already been written about them. But when we come to discuss the projection of folk and academic ideas into leisure activities, as I shall do now, we find that Sumner was quite relevant to the invention of American football. Here, as in the previous discussion of intellectual events among anthropologists, we are interested in how concepts peculiar to the folklore of capitalism have become an integral part of the games we play.

American football, of course, is derived from games played in English public schools in the Nineteenth Century. In the U.S., as in England, each school had its own rules, and oddly enough it was William Graham Sumner's son-in-law and a group of friends who wrote the rules for the Yale University version of the game (Smith 1972, Institute for the Study of Sport in Society 1971).

Several differences between Rugby and American football are notable, however. First, there is a line of scrimmage in American football and a set number of plays required to advance the ball ten yards.   Also, the offensive team proceeds by pre-planned assignments for blocking, faking, running, etc. But the difference which should interest us here is the increasing specialization of players at particular positions -- the division of labor.

Unlike Rugby, where all players are supposed to be quick and fast and run with the ball, the players of modern American football are highly specialized -- the quarterback throws, the center blocks, and the halfback runs. As an extreme case, in modern professional football, there are many players who do nothing but kick the ball in special situations.   Also, some quarterbacks do not run, and some pass receivers do not block.

It has often been noted that American football is a projection of American society (Meggyesy 1970). Vince Lombardi, for example, directly compared running a team to running an American business (1963:15). So it might be interesting to see if the ethnic and class stereotypes of Carnegie and Ford are also projected into American football.   That is, if white immigrants and later Negroes were assigned to the manual jobs in American industry, according to industrial division of labor, perhaps they also got the less intellectual roles in football.

Looking first at the role of white immigrants in football I have collected the team rosters of all the National Football League teams in 1935 and 1940, before the entry of large numbers of Negroes into the league. Then I identified East European and Italian surnames, and looked to see which positions these people were assigned to play. My hypothesis was that immigrant groups would be over represented at "muscle" positions and under represented at "brain" positions, just as they should be in American industry, according to Andrew Carnegie.

Four-hundred eleven players are represented on the team rosters. Of these, 67, or 16.3%, have Italian or East European surnames. Of the 67, 42% played at tackle or guard, "muscle" positions of the interior line. The totals by each position show that immigrant players were under represented at quarterback, halfback, and end, and over represented in the interior line and at fullback (For football fans, I should add that my sample does include Bronko Nagurski.).

Washington has done the same kind of analysis for Negro players in the 1970s (Washington 1978). My conclusions and his are presented in tabular form as follows:

Composition of Combined 1935 and 1940 NFL Teams

Positions	Aryan	Percent	Non-Aryans	Percent	Non-Aryans Overrepresented
All	346	83.7	67	16.3	
QB	25	92	2	8	
HB	81	84	13	16	
FB	29	72	8	28	X
C	35	77	8	23	X
G	61	70	18	30	X
T	54	81	10	19	X
E	61	87	8	13	

Composition of the NFL by Position
(Washington 1978)

	%Black	%White
Total Players	44.5	55.5
Center	2.0	98.0
Guard	25.3	74.7
Tackle (Offensive)	32.3	67.7
Tight End	49.4	50.6
Wide Receiver	69.0	31.0
Quarterback	5.0	95.0
Running Back	70.6	29.4
Defensive End	56.5	43.5
Defensive Tackle	42.0	58.0
Linebacker	27.5	72.5
Defensive Back	69.7	30.3
Punter	3.6	96.4
Placekicker	0.0	100.0
Coaches	3.8	96.2

In modern times, then, blacks have been "typed" at certain positions, just as white immigrants were previously, although the game is played somewhat differently now. In 1940, for example, the center did not analyze defenses and call blocking assignments, as he does now, at an "intellectual" position where 98% of the players are white. Also, NFL runners are now all "running backs", with no strong distinction between halfback (speed and finesse) and fullback (power), as in 1940.

It is also useful to note that modern coaches, who decide who plays where, are white. And it is the ethnic or racial stereotyping of the coach, his version of the folk cosmology, which is acted out by his players on the field.

The football spectators, too, can have their prejudices reinforced by seeing the same division of labor on the field as they see on the job, or that they read about in popular books. The full participant in the folk cosmology, of course, is the corporate manager who rationalizes the division of labor in his factory by reading Antony Jay, and is reassured that all races and classes are in proper cosmological order, when he sees the Rams play the Jets.

Trustworthy, Loyal and Aggressive

On the football field, however, there are no Republicans or Democrats, and no conservatives or liberals. Apparently, then, the cosmological split between conservatives and New Deal liberals cannot be observed there. But other leisure activities do demonstrate this bifurcation, especially the histories of the Boy Scouts of America and Junior Achievement, both "popular" institutions by any measure. At the present time, there are approximately forty-five million Americans who have participated in one or both of these activities.

From its beginnings in 1910, the Boy Scouts organization was closely associated with, when it was not actually sponsored by, the Federal Government (Oursler 1955, Murray 1937). The Scouts' federal charter dates from 1916, after which time an impressive array of Presidents, Senators, and Congressmen have encouraged Scout activities, and found financial support for them. American aristocrats, too, including Andrew Carnegie and John D. Rockefeller, have given time and money to American Scouting.

Because of the close ties between Scouting and the federal government, then, Franklin Roosevelt was able to use the Scouts to push his own political viewpoint, his own cosmological view of American society. Under the New Deal, 63 Scout troops were organized for Negroes by 1937, youths who were previously excluded from Scouting (Murray 1937:176). New Deal perspectives on international politics were incorporated into the "World Brotherhood" merit badge, offered soon after World War II, as well as into changed requirements for being a "First Class Scout."

Although Junior Achievement had been around since 1919, it did not attract much attention from corporate businessmen until 1938. Apparently the American business community, struggling against New Deal policies, saw Junior Achievement as an excellent vehicle for expressing their own personal values and their notions of proper politics, morality, and business ethics (JA 1978a).

By 1938, Junior Achievement had developed a program for organizing 16- to 21-year-olds into "companies" supervised by volunteer executives. The companies then collected capital, organized production of some simple commodity, and then sold their product, hopefully for a profit. In so doing, they learned business values and business skills. In microcosm, Junior Achievement tried to manifest all the characteristics that free enterprise was supposed to exhibit in the larger society.

Charles R. Hook, president of Armco Steel but also, more importantly, president of the powerful National Association of Manufacturers, recognized the public relations value of Junior Achievement in 1938 and organized a meeting of 750 business executives at the Waldorf-Astoria Hotel on December 5, 1941, to discuss expansion and financing of Junior Achievement programs. Although the development of Junior Achievement was retarded somewhat by World War II, it has now grown to offer programs in 1100 American communities. It remains under the close sponsorship of the leading "captains of industry" in the United States. Its Board of Directors includes representatives of nearly every major American company (JA 1978b).

While I do not wish to dwell at any length on a comparison and contrast of the Scouts and Junior Achievement, it is interesting to contrast the values expressed in their respective public slogans, and find patterns of agreement between them and the cosmologies of Carnegie and Roosevelt. For example, all of us who have been Scouts (I must confess, as a participant observer, that I was an Eagle Scout) know that Scouts are trustworthy, loyal, helpful, friendly, courteous, kind, obedient, cheerful, thrifty, brave, clean and reverent. But why aren't scouts supposed to be "intelligent", and why aren't they "aggressive." These traits, which writers such as Carnegie, Sumner, Rand and Tiger have said are of central importance and immutable to boot, are missing from the list.

But such characteristics are discussed at length in the literature of Junior Achievement. Once again we are on familiar ground here, finding an endorsement of "innovation, mobility, early responsibility, personal achievement and entrepreneurship (Dateline 10:2, p. 6), along with "pride" and "enthusiasm." By contrast with these Junior Achievement traits of character, the values promoted by the Boy Scouts seem rural and arcane, familial or collective rather than individualistic. And these are the same value differences which have separated liberals and conservatives in American political life (Turner and Starnes 1967:68-73).

Our cosmological circle can be closed, then, by reference to a man who is not only the ideological descendent of Henry Ford, but a biological descendent as well. In his address to Junior Achievement in 1978, Henry Ford II, after complaining again about government "interference" in business affairs, said (Dateline 11:2, p. 3):

> I can't praise the Junior Achievement program too highly. . .Young people who have had some exposure to economics invariably develop a better understanding of the complex problems that an economic system has to deal with and a much better appreciation of the remarkable capabilities of our private enterprise system. Now if the majority of the American people eventually develop an understanding of how our economic system works, and what is needed to keep it productive, we will no longer have to worry about the golden goose becoming an endangered species. . .You can carry the word that it is time for our society to reexamine its economic priorities.

Conclusions

Anthropologists frequently congratulate themselves on having a holistic approach to the study of culture. Instead of sorting out the events in a tribal society into politics, family, personality, and economics and then studying only one topic, anthropologists most often try to understand everything at once. They are interested in how certain aspects of culture, for example "kinship" in a tribal society, are reflected in all varieties of actual behavior. The price one pays for being holistic, however, is that most aspects of culture are treated very superficially.

Of the topics mentioned in this essay, obviously volumes have been written or could have been written about each one. A thorough comparison of the Boy Scouts and Junior Achievement, tracing their histories and comparing their values, would take years of work of the sort already begun by Nicholson (1941) or Hoyt (1978). Similarly, a critical history of the Carnegie Institutions would necessitate months of library research to offer reliable conclusions about patterns of funding and motivations for research. So what possible excuse can I offer for treating these complicated subjects in such a seemingly casual manner.

In his introduction to Culture Against Man, Jules Henry remarked (1963:4):

Whereas in primitive culture the anthropologist often has to work to ferret out information, in our great democracy the printing presses inundate him with it, and his greatest task is to sort it out and interpret it.

So what has my goal been in selecting certain episodes from American society and discussing them, while neglecting others?

In brief, my purpose has been to take three steps back from American culture and point out some important congruencies which exist among apparently disparate aspects of culture. These congruencies, I assert, are mostly invisible to the participants in the culture. If I were to suggest, for example, to a Boy Scout leader, that he was fulfilling the political charter of the New Deal, he would no doubt be baffled by my statement. Or if I were to suggest to Edward Wilson that he was firmly in the lists of the proponents of Carnegie's cosmology, that might puzzle him. In the same way, however, I have puzzled Cheyennes by suggesting that coyote skins imply male principles, while yellow earth implies female ones (Moore 1979). And I would be met with disbelief if I tried to convince a Mexican town mayor, beset by the expenses of his office, that he was being "levelled" by his townsmen (Moore 1975).

So that is the way we anthropologists flatter ourselves. We assert that our once-over-lightly approach lays bare the general structure of society in a way that studies in depth cannot do. So here in this essay I have argued that there are cosmological models of American society carried about in the heads of aristocrats and expressed in their words. I argue that aristocrats have organized real manifestations of these models among real people when they could. And I have assembled a small but solid collection of evidence that shows the structure of these models and how they are congruent among verbal, work, and leisure activities.

Bibliography

Ardrey, Robert
    1961   African Genesis, London: Collins.
    1966   The Territorial Imperative, New York: Atheneum.
    1970   The Social Contract, New York: Atheneum.

Asbell, Bernard
    1973   The F. D. R. Memoirs, New York: Doubleday.

Arnold, Thurman W.
    1937   The Folklore of Capitalism, New Haven: Yale University Press.

Baltzell, E. Digby
    1964   The Protestant Establishment, New York: Vintage.

Birmingham, Stephen
    1968   The Right People, Boston: Little, Brown.

Boas, Franz
    1912   "Changes in Bodily Form of Descendants of Immigrants" in Boas 1940:60-75.
    1931   "Race and Progress," in Boas 1940:3-17.
    1940   Race, Language, and Culture, New York: Free Press.

Boyer, Richard O. and Herbert M. Morais
    1955   Labor's Untold Story, New York: United Electrical, Radio and Machine Workers.

Brace, C. Loring and G. R. Gamble and J. T. Bond
    1971   Race and Intelligence, American Anthropological Association, Anthropological Studies No. 8.

Briffault, Robert
    1935   "Why They Are So Dumb" in Briffault 1936:51-60.
    1936   Reasons for Anger, New York: Simon and Schuster.

Carnegie, Andrew
   1893   Triumphant Democracy, New York: Scribner's.
   1902   The Empire of Business, New York: Doubleday.

Carroll, Charles
   1968   The Negro. . .A Beast or in the Image of God,
             Savannah, Georgia: The Thunderbolt, Inc.

Cole, Fay-Cooper
   1931   Obituary   of   George   Dorsey,   American
             Anthropologist 33:413-14.

Conklin, Harold C.
   1955   "Hanunoo   Color   Categories,"   Journal   of
             Anthropology 11:339-44.

Cromwell, James H. R. and Hugo E. Czerwosky
   1937   In Defense of Capitalism, New York: Scribner's
             Sons.

Darwin, Charles
   1859   Origin   of   Species,   New   York: New   American
             Library (1958).

Dateline
   The magazine of Junior Achievement, Stamford, Connecticut.

Davenport, C.B. and Morris Steggerda
   1929   Race Crossing in Jamaica, Carnegie Institution of
             Washington.

Dorsey, George
   1925   Why   We   Behave   Like   Human   Beings,   New
             York: Harper.
   1929   Hows   and   Whys   of   Human   Behavior,   New
             York: Harper.

Ford, Henry
   1923   My Life and Work, New York: Doubleday.
   1926   Today and Tomorrow, New York: Doubleday, Page.
   1930   Moving Forward, New York: Doubleday, Doran.

Franklin, Benjamin
   1944   The   Autobiography   of   Benjamin   Franklin,   New
             York: The Modern Library.

Georgakas, Dan and Marvin Surkin
   1975   Detroit-I Do Mind Dying, New York: St. Martin.

Getty, J. Paul
1971   How   to   be   a   Successful   Executive, Chicago: Playboy Press.

Greenspan, Alan
1967   "Antitrust" in Rand 1967.

Henry, Jules
1963   Culture Against Man, New York: Random House.

Hofstadter, Richard
1944   Social   Darwinism   in   American   Thought, Boston: Beacon.

Hopkins, Harry
1936   Spending to Save, New York: Norton.

Hoyt, Kenneth B.
1978   "Junior Achievement, Inc. and Career Education." U.S. Office of Education, June.

Institute for the Study of Sport in Society
1971   "The Origins of American Football," unpublished ms.

Jaffe, Philip J.
1975   The Rise and Fall of American Communism, New York: Horizon.

Jay, Antony
1972   Corporation Man, London: Jonathan Cape.

Junior Achievement
1978a   History   of   Junior   Achievement,   Memo   dated March.
1978b   Who's   Who   in   Junior   Achievement   Leadership, 1978-79, Folder F-535.

Lombardi, Vince
1963   Run to Daylight, New York: Prentice-Hall.

Lysenko, Trofim
1948   The   Science   of   Biology   Today,   New York: International Publishers.

Mannheim, Karl
1956   Essays   on   the   Sociology   of   Culture, London: Routledge and Kegan Paul.

Meggyesy, Dave
1970   Out of Their League, San Francisco: Ramparts
            Press.

Montagu, Ashley
1945   "Intelligence of Northern Negroes and Southern
            Whites in the First World War," The American
            Journal of Psychology 58:161-188.
1975   Race and IQ, Oxford University Press.

Moore, John H.
1972   The Imperialist Roots of American Anthropology,
            Paper presented to Toronto meetings of the
            American Anthropological Association.
1975   "Illegal Aliens: The View From a Mexican Village,"
            Proceedings of the Central States Anthropological
            Society, edited by Gustaf Carlson.
1979   "The Utility of Cheyenne Cosmology," Papers in
            Anthropology 20:2.

Muller, H. J.
1935   Out of the Night, New York: Harper.

Murray, William D.
1937   The History of the Boy Scouts of America,
            Published by BSA.

Nicholson, Edwin
1941   Education and the Boy Scout Movement in
            America, New York: Columbia University
            Teachers College.

Opler, Morris E.
1945   Themes as Dynamic Forces in Culture, American
            Journal of Sociology 51:198-206.

Otten, Allen L.
1974   "Politics and People", Wall Street Journal, March 7,
            p. 14, col. 3.

Ousler, Will
1955   The Boy Scout Story, New York: Doubleday.

Proletariat
1979   "A Re-Examination of the Lysenko Controversy in
            the Soviet Union," Proletariat 5:1, pp. 32-44.

Radin, Paul
1957   Primitive Man as Philosopher, New York: Dover.

Rand, Ayn
1967   Capitalism: the Unknown Ideal, New American Library.
1964   The Virtue of Selfishness, New York: New American Library.

Reiter, Rayna R.
1975   Toward an Anthropology of Women, New York: Monthly Review Press.

Rodenwalt, E.
1927   Die Mestizen auf Kisar, Batavia (2 vol.).

Roosevelt, Eleanor
1961   Autobiography, New York: Harper.

Roosevelt, Franklin D.
1934   On Our Way, New York: John Day.

Rosaldo, Michelle and Louise Lamphere
1974   Woman, Culture and Society, Stanford University Press.

Sahlins, Marshall
1976   The Use and Abuse of Biology, University of Michigan Press.

Shuey, A.
1966   The Testing of Negro Intelligence, New York: Social Science Press.

Smith, W. Robertson
1882   The Prophets of Israel, New York: Appleton.

Smith, Robert
1972   Illustrated History of Pro Football, New York: Grosset and Dunlap.

Snyder, Carl
1940   Capitalism the Creator, New York: Macmillan.

Starobin, Joseph R.
1972   American Communism in Crisis, 1943-1957, University of California Press.

Stern, Bernhard J.
1949   "Human Heredity and Environment," in B. Stern 1959:316-327.
1950   "Does Genetic Endowment Vary by Socioeconomic Group" in Science 111:697-8, June 23.

1959   Historical Sociology, New York: Citadel.

Stern, Curt
   1948   Principles of Human Genetics, W. H. Freeman.

Stocking, George W.
   1968   Race, Culture and Evolution, New York: Free
             Press.

Tiger, Lionel
   1969   Men in Groups, New York: Holt, Rinehart and
             Winston.

Tiger, Lionel and Robin Fox
   1971   The Imperial Animal, New York: Holt, Rinehart
             and Winston.

Turner, Jonathan and Charles Starnes
   1976   Inequality: Privilege and Poverty in America,
             Pacific Palisades, California: Goodyear.

Washington, Michael
   1978   The Locker Room is a Ghetto, Equal Rights
             Congress, P. O. Box 2488, Chicago, Illinois 60690.

Weber, Max
   1930   The Protestant Ethic, New York: Scribner's.

Wilson, Edward O.
   1978   On Human Nature, Harvard University Press.

Withers, Hartley
   1920   The Case for Capitalism, New York: Dutton.

4. Toward a More Biological Psychology

The pendulum of scientific explanation swings from reductionism to superordination, from explaining too little to explaining too much. In the 1920s, psychology appealed to the biological sciences for help. By the '30s, political changes favored reliance on the more social sciences. An aversion to biological determinism persisted into the '60s. In more recent years, I think there is a decided swing back to biology. As a developmental psychologist concerned with genetic differences in behavior, I hardly despise the shift; in fact, I feel better understood with each passing year. But I am also concerned about the excessive zeal with which biological notions are being received in psychology today, and, more painfully, with some of the misconceptions that uncritical adoption can bring.

I want to review some of the historical shifts in psychological preferences for levels of explanation, with an eye to not repeating historical mistakes.

Each generation of psychologists rediscovers the nature-nurture problem. Contemporary students of the issue have been handicapped, however, by a chasm in intellectual history between the present group of middle-aged behavioral scientists, who ruled the issue out of polite discourse, and older generations of scholars who actually did research on the problem. Those of us who were educated in the 1950s and early 1960s were taught, for the most part, an environmentalism-run-amok. From the mid-1960s, the nature-nurture problem took on new life, but, alas, few of us were in contact with the wisdom of earlier generations.

To rediscover what used to be widely known about nature and nurture, let us examine some wisdom from Woodworth's classic book (1941).

These two statements--(1) that differences in
environment can produce substantial differences in
intelligence, and (2) that differences actually present in a community are not due mostly to differences
in environment--may appear mutually contradictory.
That they are not contradictory has been emphatically pointed out by several students of the nature-
nurture problem. For example:

Shuttleworth (1935): "The data of Burks indicate very clearly that inter-family environmental
differences account for a much smaller proportion...
of the variance...in intelligence than do hereditary
differences.... The inferiority complex which many
educators and environmentalists have created for
themselves by the misinterpretation of these and
similar data is a most bizarre phenomenon. It does
not follow that the general level of the environment is a relatively unimportant factor in determining the general level of intelligence, but only
that environmental differences are relatively small
in comparison with hereditary differences in determining individual differences in intelligence.
Even if environmental differences accounted for zero
percent, and hereditary differences accounted for
100 percent of the individual differences in intelligence, it would still be true that the general
level of the environment would be a most important
factor determining the general level of intelligence."

Although Woodworth and Shuttleworth directed their comments
to intelligence, the same principles apply to all human behavior; i.e., learning, personality, social behavior, and so
forth. The determinants of differences in behavior are not
necessarily the determinants of development. This is the
first issue I want to address. The second issue is malleability, and the third is individual versus group differences.
Last, I want to review some of the recent findings of family
studies on the sources of individual and group differences
in behavior, especially as they illuminate the effects of
variations in our rearing environments.

Differences Versus Development

For mysterious reasons, there is quite a psychological
literature that asserts that it is useless to try to separate
the effects of genes and environments as sources of human
differences because both are required for development. This
statement is a second rate non-sequitor. Of course, both
genes and environment are required to program the development

of the organism, including behavioral development. It is no accident that all human brains and behaviors have more in common with each other than any human has with any other species. Ernst Mayr (1970) has eloquently described an evolved genetic program for development that is largely shared by all species members. Individual differences among us are minor variations on the species theme.

YK

⌐Individual differences may arise from these minor variations in our genetic program, and they may arise from differences in our rearing environments. As Waddington, the great British biologist, has pointed out, development is the process by which genotypes come to be expressed as observable phenotypes, including behavioral phenotypes. For a genotype to be expressed, an environment is required. Differences in those environments may create differences in even the same genotype, although for many purposes variations in our environments may only be apparent differences without substantial effects, a theme I will return to later. At present, the major point is that either genetic differences or environmental differences or both—during development—are responsible for the varied behaviors we observe. Whereas both are required for development to occur at all, either or both may cause differences among individuals.⌐

Malleability

YK

⌐There is another mysterious myth abroad in the land concerning the fixed effects of genes on what we observe and measure. "If it's genetic (whatever that menas), it cannot be changed." Nonsense! As we all know from the psychological literature and from personal experience, big changes in environments, especially from deprived or abusive ones to environments in the normal range, have big effects on children's behavior. Recent reevaluations of Head Start (Zigler, 1977; Palmer, 1977) now show substantial effects of the program on later learning. Arthur Jensen (1977) has recently shown that the rural Southern environment of many Blacks produces a substantial, cumulative deficit in their intellectual functioning. Since development is controlled by both the genetic program and the environment, then changes in one or the other can alter the course of development. Behavioral changes that occur in response to environmental changes we usually call malleability or plasticity in development.⌐

Finding genetic sources of individual differences in behavior does not imply that environmental changes will have little or no effect. When genetic differences among individuals account for, let's say, half of the variance, then redistributing the environments that were actually sampled in

the study can have huge effects. More importantly, introducing new environments or those that were not sampled can have
unlimited effects.

In another brief return to the wisdom of the past, listen
to what Edward Thorndike said in 1914: "...Many disagree-
ments spring from a confusion of what may be called absolute
achievement with what may be called relative achievement. A
man may move up a long distance from zero and nevertheless be
lower down than before in comparison with other men who have
moved up still farther. The commonest error...is that of
concluding from the importance of...heredity that education
and social control in general are futile....To the real
work of man for man--the increase of achievement through
improvement of the the environment--the influence of heredity
offers no barrier." (Woodworth, pp. 30-31).

As Thorndike clearly understood, levels of behavioral
development are malleable. Improvements in environments
will improve phenotypes. And he also highlighted a second
principle of malleability: that individuals respond differently to those improvements. Individuals, we now believe,
have genetically different responses to similar environments.
This genetically-different responsiveness has been called
the range of reaction. As Irving Gottesman (1963) has explained it, range of reaction means that each individual has
a range of possible developmental responses to a range of
environments (in other words, each of us will have better or
worse phenotypes, depending on our environments), but different people will not show the same response to the same environment. Malleability does not that we will all end up
alike. Common sense and a lot of animal studies with different strains and breeds confirm this same principle.

Thus, there are two principles of malleability: (1) that
genes do not fix behavior, but establish a range of probable
responses to environments, and (2) that individuals vary
in their repertory of possible developmental responses.
Thus, the level of performance or adjustment, or whatever,
is responsive to the environments in which people are reared,
and yet individuals will still differ from others reared in
similar environments.

Now, let me add two aspects of an evolutionary view of
human behavior: first, the socio-cultural context in which
human brains and behavior evolved and developed; and second,
the necessary genetic implications of an evolutionary view.
Many other sources provide a more complete and scholarly account of these issues (e.g., Mayr, 1970, 1974; Dobzhansky,
1962, 1973), but I want to set the stage for a discussion of
the returning biological emphasis in psychology.

We are compromise organisms. The evolution of behavior cannot be separated from all of the other characteristics that make us viable, functioning beings in our human environments. Brains and behavior had to be co-adapted with reproductive requirements, life-span limitations, motor functions, etc.

Every genetic change, as Mayr (1970) has pointed out, must be fitted into the existing genetic program, rather more like adding a violin to an orchestra than expecting a solo performance. The final arrangement of instruments is that which makes the best adapted compromise with all of the requirements of the environment, without unduly favoring one function over any others that are necessary for survival and reproduction. So, brains and behavior could not evolve willy-nilly without being part of the co-adapted gene complex that determines all of the organisms' development.

In each generation there is a feedback system for genetic change. Individuals are more or less successful at procreating and rearing their offspring to reproductive age. Since the gene pool of the next generation depends on the frequency of successful reproduction of the parental genotypes, differential fertility and mortality of the preceding generation will directly determine the genetic character of the next.

Through most of human history both differential fertility and mortality changed the gene pool from one generation to the next. Some people were more desirable as mates than others, some produced more offspring, and some were more successful in parenting those offspring to adulthood, when the parental genes could extend into yet another generation. As long as genetic differences in behavior had even the slightest part in this drama of human fertility and mortality, some genes would be increased and others decreased in frequency over time. It may be noted here that in the 20th century, differential mortality of parents and offspring has decreased as an evolutionary factor because most babies now survive to reproductive age in most of the world. (This is not to say that public health and infant mortality are no longer issues even in the United States, but that differential mortality by nation, class, race, and probably IQ level have all declined.) Differential fertility, on the other hand, has increased for the moment, as the more modernized and affluent were the first to deliberately limit family size effectively. It is still quite likely, however, that human intelligence is holding its own, with the more intelligent in every group outreproducing the retarded by a slight margin, as in the U.S. white population (Higgins, Reed and Reed, 1962;

Bajema, 1968). Fertility is a volatile measure, however, as
more and more peoples around the world achieve some measure
of reproductive control.

Because some behaviors, such as human intelligence,
evolved by directional selection toward bigger brains, symbolic thought, and more complex communication, there must be
a genetic basis for the development of these behaviors to
account for the regular appearance of intellectual changes in
childhood. The species genetic program must include a timed
turning-on of the capacity to acquire these skills. There
may also be a timed turning-off of the easy learning of some
skills, as Lenneberg (1967) found for primary language acquisition.

With the exception of a few severely impaired individuals,
all human beings have more in common with each other than with
any other species. This is one way to say that individual
differences within the species are very small compared to
our differences from even our closest relatives. Variations
in the developmental genetic program are not so large as to
allow any human child to resemble a chimp more than another
child. Even severely isolated children do not resemble great
apes; such children are sadly deficient in human or any other
skills. And a chimp reared in a human environment does not
become a human child. So, to become a functioning human being
clearly requires both the species genetic program and a rearing environment within the range that was evolutionarily typical for the species. However platitudinous, this fact is too
often debated by the cold warriors of the nature-nurture controversy.

Since there is a species genetic program for behavioral
development, there is also very likely to be genetic variability for behavior; that is, individual differences that depend
in part on genotypic differences. Certainly, during the mil-
lions of years of human evolution, selection acted on genetic
variability or there would have been no evolutionary change.
That there was change is demonstrated by the fossil record.

Some geneticists, including Lewontin, question whether
there is any variance left for behavior in contemporary populations. Maybe it was all used up in our struggle to become Homo sapiens, an achievement of the last 50,000 years.
Studies of sibling differences, adopted children, and twins
deny this speculation. Within every group studied, there is
genetic variability in behavior. I will return to this point
later.

If one is either convinced or willing to assume for the
sake of argument that there is some genetic variance for

behavior left in contemporary human populations, then the
more profitable question is how is that variance likely to
be affected by variations in the environment? Are all of the
possible combinations of genes and environments likely to
produce linear increases or decreases--so much of a linear
slope for genetic differences, so much for environmental differences?

Some obscurantists (e.g., Hirsch, 1975), who think that
questions about genetic differences are either unanswerable
or immoral, have argued that gene-environment interactions
(non-linear effects) produce wild discontinuities in the phenotypes produced by various gene-environment combinations.
Are there really genotypes that flourish in less humane, less
invigorating environments? Poor Jake, if only he had had
less protein and fewer books in childhood, he'd be a genius
today instead of just a little above average. Lucky Sal,
her parents gave her just the right amount of abuse and neglect to optimally foster her low IQ. Is this likely? I
suppose that within the normal limits on nutrition, opportunities to learn, adult stimulation, etc., some genotypes would
develop better with less rather than more. But are these
large effects? I would guess that the discontinuities produced by such combinations produce a little static on the
linear regression of gene-environment combinations.

The development of these typically human skills depends
both on evolved biases in learning that make it easier to acquire some skills than others and proper environmental conditions for development. Once one considers the nction that
human intelligence evolved in the socio-cultural context of
small human groups, of mixed ages and sexes, who traveled
around gathering food and sometimes hunting, one can begin
to question the implications of this environment for the
kinds of human intelligence that evolved. And one can look
at the pan-human context for intellectual development (e.g.,
Scarr-Salapatek, 1976). Some environmental conditions are
very generally available for all members of the human species,
such as opportunities to communicate with others, to manipulate objects, and to move about in space. Children cannot
learn any language without its being present in their environments, nor can they learn to locomote in space without the
opportunity to do so. But all normal, humane environments
provide these opportunities. More particular environments
may be required for the development of literacy, such as formal instruction in reading and writing skills (see Cole, Gay,
Glick and Sharpe, 1971). But the human species has evolved
to be capable of acquiring such skills with the provision of
requisite environmental supports. Even those children in
groups that only recently acquired writing readily learn

literacy skills. The major point is that environments of almost all groups not undergoing disasters from plague, star-
vation, or war provide the necessary opportunities and instruction for the young to acquire the local culture and to
develop into species-typical human beings.

Is the Genetic Program Sensitive to
Environmental Variations?

Several remarkable cases of extreme isolation in early
childhood have been reported and reviewed recently by the
Clarkes (Clarke and Clarke, 1976). Isolated children, when
discovered around the ages of 6 or 7, were extremely retarded in their intellectual development, having been reared
in environments that deviated disastrously from those of
normal members of the species. These children had little or
no exposure to language, opportunities for sensorimotor development, or interpersonal affection. Like cage-reared,
isolated monkeys, they were sadly deficient in the usual
childhood skills, until patient tutoring and exposure over
the next few years succeeded in bringing all but one (the
famous Anna, reported by Kingsley Davis) up to average levels
of intellectual performance. There is no question that being reared in environments outside the range that is normal
for the species will have deleterious consequences.

Environments outside the optimal range, at the margins
of those that are normal for the species, can also have measurable, deleterious effects. Poor protein-calorie nutrition,
cultural isolation (such as that of the canal-boat children
in England and the Appalachian children of the 1930s), being reared in an unstimulating institution and not attending
school for at least a few years, all seem to depress intellectual functioning, as measured by both Western IQ test and
more culturally suitable assessments (Cole et al., 1971).

As a species, our developmental program is best suited
to profiting from the learning and problem solving opportunities that occur in some rather broad range of human environments. Peoples around the world do not rear children in the
same ways. The many variations on caretaking (who does it?),
cultural patterns of sleeping and eating (what, with whom,
and when?), food production or gathering, are the delight of
cultural anthropologists. But are there any societies where
children are typically excluded from interacting with other
speakers of the human language, refused opportunities to ex-
plore material objects, and denied opportunities to learn the
culture into which they have been born?

My conclusion is that children around the world develop
typically human skills because their genetic programs for

development are very similar and their environments are functionally equivalent for the development of typical human skills.

Racial Versus Socioeconomic Groups
Within the U.S.

More than 40 years ago, Davis and Dollard (1937) contrasted the social systems of caste and class. Among castes there is no individual mobility; one is born into a caste and stays there regardless of individual merit. Races are castes in the U.S. Social classes exist within castes, and individuals can move up or down the class structure according to criteria of individual merit. Dobzhansky (1962) spelled out the implications of this differentiation for genetics: Genetic differences are less likely to arise between castes because all of the genetic individual variability is kept within them--there are few ways out of one racial group into another. By contrast, there are permeable boundaries among social class groups, not perfect mobility according to individual merit, but some 30 to 40% changes of status in each generation. The individuals who move socially take their genes with them, mate, and reproduce in their achieved status. Thus, there is a far higher probability of social class than racial group differences in those characteristics that contribute to individual mobility (Scarr-Salapatek, 1971a, 1971b).

The implication of the differences between race and social class for intellectual achievement is that there are more likely to be genetic differences in IQ scores between social class than racial groups. Let us review the recent research on this issue.

The Evidence on Racial Differences as
Environment and Genes

Three recent investigations on the possible genetic origins of racial differences in performance in school and on IQ tests reject the hypothesis of genetic differences as a major source of those differences in performance. First, a study of transracial adoption (Scarr and Weinberg, 1976) showed that Black and interracial children reared by socioeconomically advantaged White families score very well on standard IQ tests and on school achievement tests. Being reared in the culture of the test and the schools resulted in intellectual achievement levels for Black children that were comparable to adopted Caucasian children in similar families. Therefore, it is highly unlikely that genetic differences between the races could account for the major portion of the usually observed differences in the performance levels of the two groups.

A second study on the relation of Black ancestry to intellectual skills within the Black population (Scarr, Pakstis,
Katz and Barker, 1977) showed that having more or less African
ancestry was not related to how well one scored on cognitive
tests. In other words, holding constant social identity and
cultural background, socially classified Blacks with greater
amounts of White ancestry did not score better than other
Blacks with more African ancestry. A strong genetic difference hypothesis cannot account for this result.

Briefly, blood groups were used to estimate the proportion of each person's African and European ancestry. This is
roughly possible because the parent populations differ in the
average frequency of many alleles and differ substantially at
a few loci. Therefore, if a person has a particular allele,
we were able to assign a probability that he got that gene
from one of the two populations. While there is undoubtedly
a large error term in these estimates, they had several satisfactory characteristics, such as appropriately large sibling
correlations and correlations with skin color. What is important here is that the estimates of ancestry did not corre-
late with any measures of intellectual performance in the
Black sample. Thus, we concluded that degree of White ancestry had little or no effect on individual levels of performance within the Black group. We must look to other explanations.

The third study was of Black and White twins in Philadelphia (Scarr and Barker, 1978). Briefly, the Black 10- to
16-year-olds scored half to one standard deviation below the
Whites on every cognitive measure. The social class differences between the races were not sufficiently large, as
Jensen has reminded us, to account solely for the magnitude
of this performance difference between the racial groups.
The major hypothesis was that Black children have less overall familiarity with the information and the skills being
sampled by the tests and the schools. By using twins in
this study, we were able to examine three implications of
cultural differences compared to a genetic difference hypothesis.

We believe that the pattern of results supports a general
cultural difference hypothesis far better than a genetic
difference view. The major results of tests designed to measure intellectual levels are:

1. Black children have lower scores on all of the cognitive tests, but they score relatively worse on the
more culturally-loaded of the conceptual tests.

2. The cognitive differences among the Black children are less well explained by genetic individual differences, by age and by social class differences than those of the White children.

3. The similarity of the Black co-twins, particularly the dizygotic ones, suggests that being reared in different families determines more of the cognitive differences among Black than White children, but that those between-family differences are not those usually measured by SES variables in the White community.

Therefore, we conclude that the results of this study support the view that Black children are being reared in circumstances that give them only marginal acquaintance with the skills and the knowledge being sampled by the tests we administered. Some families in the Black community encourage the development of these skills and knowledge while others do not. In general, Black children do not have the same access to these skills and knowledge as White children, which explains the lower performance of Black children as a group. The hypothesis that most of the differences among the cognitive scores of Black and White children are due to genetic differences between the races cannot, in our view, account for this pattern of results. Therefore, in three studies the hypothesis of genetic differences between the races fails to account for the IQ performance differences.

The Evidence on Individual Differences as Genes and Environments

From a review of recent family studies (Scarr, 1977), I think that the evidence for some genetic individual differences in behavior is simply overwhelming. Especially if one considers the past literature, there are literally dozens of studies that support that mild conclusion in all groups studied.

Going straight to the heart of the matter, I think that most evidence points to a "heritability" of about .4 to .7 in the U.S. White population and .2 to .5 in the Black, given that "heritability" here means the proportion of genetic variance among individuals sampled in twin and family studies, which as I have repeatedly noted are not representative of bad environments. If one could include people with really poor environments, the proportion of environmental variance might rise; on the other hand, the genetic variance might also be increased. It is hard to predict whether the proportions of variance would change or not, and in which direction.

It is important to note here the small effects of environmental differences on IQ scores among the people in our
samples of White adoptive and biologically related families.
This suggests that within the range of "humane environments",
from an SES level of working to upper middle class, there is
little evidence for differential environmental effects within
the whole group. The average level of these environments is
such that the Black and White children reared by these families perform intellectually somewhat above the population average, even though they have average biological parents. Thus,
the environments sampled in family studies are better than
average at fostering intellectual development. But why are
the relatively poor families rearing Black and White adopted
children whose IQ scores are nearly as high as those in professional families? It must be that all of these seeming
environmental differences that predict so well as to outcome
differences among biological children are not primarily environmental differences, but indices of genetic differences
among the parents and their biological offspring. This brings
us to social class.

The Evidence on Social Class Differences as
Environments and Genes

In 1938, Barbara Burks compared her California-adopted
and biological children to those studies by Alice Leahy in
Minnesota. Grouping the children by the occupational status
of the adoptive families, Burks computed the average effects
of being born to and reared by, or only reared by, families
at different locations in the social structure. As in all
adoption studies, the families do not vary over the whole
SES range; in fact, adoptive samples always omit those lower
portions of the income and educational distributions where
big negative effects on intellectual development can occur.
Nonetheless, it is interesting to examine the overall effects
of being reared by a skilled working class family, or a white
collar family, or a professional family. As you already
know, intellectual levels of parents in those groups differ
on the average. What about the children?

For biological children of these occupational classes,
the average difference between working class and professional
families was 12 IQ points in Burks' study and 17 IQ points
in Leahy's. Children adopted by families of the same occupational classes, however, differed far less--about 5 IQ
points in both studies. Adopted children in professional
families scored below biological offspring; in working class
families, adoptees scored above the natural children, a very
predictable genetic outcome.

It should be noted that the genetic prediction for the IQ scores of adoptive children, compared to biological offspring of the same or similar families, is based on random assignment of genotypically bright and dull adoptees to families at all locations in the social structure. Although this is not a perfect assumption, because agencies selectively place infants of educationally-advanced natural mothers with adoptive families of higher educational levels (and lower with lower), the effects on IQ resemblance between adoptive parents and their children is small, because educational level is an imperfect estimator of IQ scores of the adoptive parents, and natural mother's educational level is certainly a distal estimate of the genetic contribution of both natural parents to their offspring's eventual intellectual level. Therefore, the genetic prediction is that children adopted into professional families will be environmentally advantaged but genotypically average, whereas the biological offspring of the same or similar parents will be both environmentally and genotypically advantaged. Similarly, the children adopted by working class families will be environmentally less advantaged but genotypically average, whereas the children born into such families will be both environmentally and genotypically disadvantaged. Selective placement of the adoptive children works against the genetic prediction.

In our Minnesota studies (Scarr and Weinberg, 1976, 1977, and Scarr, 1977), we found that the natural children of the transracial adoptive families averaged 6 IQ points above their adopted siblings. The adolescent adoptees also average 6 IQ points below the biological children of comparably advantaged families. As in other studies, there is a far greater relationship between parental social class and child IQ in the biological than adoptive families.

Since there is always some selective placement of adopted children into families that resemble their biological parents, the actual effect of differences in this middle to high range of social class environments may be less than the 5 or 6 IQ points cited. Again, let me emphasize that none of these studies speak to lower-class, deprived, or abusive environments. I am only saying that in that portion of the SES range where so many studies report intellectual differences among children reared in such circumstances that the differences observed among the children may not be primarily of environmental origin at all. From the older studies, Burks estimated that genetic differences among the occupational classes account for about 2/3 to 3/4 of the average IQ differences among the children born into those classes. Our recent studies support that conclusion.

Why Study Genetic Differences in Behavior?

It may occur to some of you that the shift to a biological emphasis in psychology is pessimistic. What's left to the systematic environment? (There's a lot left to random events or otherwise unexplained!)

I do not see these research outcomes as pessimistic in the slightest. On the contrary, I think a more realistic appreciation of biological effects will permit behavioral scientists and social policy makers to sort out important differences in people's environments. There are three major reasons that I think behavior genetic studies of families are useful.

The first, and weakest one for social policy, is terribly important to many of us. That is, we need to gain a fuller understanding of the nature of human behavior. The naive environmentalism of the past three decades locked us into assumptions that are simply untenable, useless, and wrongheaded. The average layman had better intuitions about the nature of human differences than many psychologists purported to have. I have a sneaky suspicion, however, that most psychologists privately explained behavioral differences much as the rest of the population does. But why should we continue to be publicly wrong?

The second reason for behavior genetic studies of families is more "relevant", to use a phrase of the '60s. These studies can and do provide diagnostic clues about the nature of some developmental problems. Just as a good family history in medicine and clinical psychology expresses a concern for individual risks, so tracing family patterns of behaviors affords us a look at human behavior in the making, and often a more optimistic prognosis. So, father was a "hyperactive boy"; today he is a successful businessman. So, when mother was a child, she had a difficult time meeting new people; today she is a respected member of community groups. Psychologists can afford to have more respect for the individual patterns of development that make us different from one another. Biological diversity is a fact of life; respect for individual differences comes very much from that biological perspective and is not a trivial victory.

Third, and most important to me, are the implications for intervention programs. In its baldest form, I think that naive environmentalism has led us into an "intervention fallacy". By assuming that all of the variance in behavior was environmentally determined, we have blithely promised a world of change that we have not delivered, at great cost to the

participants, the public and ourselves. The fallacy runs
like this: if people who do X without our intervention have
more desirable outcomes than people who do not do X, then
we should persuade, or compel, all people to do X. This is
illogical and unwise, because some of the reasons for the
naturally occurring differences between those who do and do
not do X are not just environmental differences. I argue
that many of these seemingly environmental variations are
actually genetic differences or gene-environment correlations.
People who are different do things differently.

But here is the most costly part of the intervention
fallacy: the erroneous belief that small variations in environments within the "humane range" have meaningfully different outcomes for children. If we observe that professional families take their children to the theatre more often than working class families, or hang mobiles above their
cribs more frequently, some psychologists feel justified in
recommending to everyone that they take in plays frequently,
rather than playing baseball in the back yard, or hang mobiles over the crib, rather than carrying the baby about
wherever the parents go. Since these are the child-rearing
practices of the professional class, whose children excel at
IQ tests and in school, some psychologists would advise all
parents to alter their child-rearing practices to follow
suit. It has not been demonstrated that these variations in
child-rearing are functionally different in their effects on
the children; I argue that most "humane environments" are in
fact functionally equivalent. But the load of guilt and the
financial burden placed on parents has been extraordinary,
based on studies of the naturally occurring variation among
families and the outcome of their biological offspring. Behavior genetic studies of families can spare us all a homogeneity of environmental practices, imposed by an omniscient
professional class.

I believe that we can do a better job of designing and
implementing effective intervention programs if we know what
variations in the environment make a difference and which
ones do not. We can shift our resources to the improvement
of those circumstances that have clear, environmentally-dele-
terious effects on people. Many of these we know: we do
not have to do research to know that hunger is bad for children, or that child abuse leaves scars. Most of the worst
environments are obviously deleterious. But there are many
other marginal and less obvious conditions that we can only
judge from sophisticated research on the effects of these environments. So, it is important to know what aspects of the
environment have consequences for behavioral differences and
which ones are only apparent variations, based on cultural

preferences, genetic differences or on gene-environment correlations. People deserve respect for self-expression and their
own modes of child-rearing, unless there is clear environmental reason to intervene. Behavior genetic methods will
help us to gain a far clearer understanding of which environmental variables to worry about.

But, let us recall the wisdom of the past: as Thorndike
and others said, the average level of our environment is the
most important determinant of the level of behavioral development. Therefore, by providing better schooling, nutrition,
health care, psychological services and the like, we can raise
the average level of the environment and of behavioral development in the whole population.

Scientific evidence on individual and group differences
does not speak to the issue of average levels, nor does such
research have any implications for the distribution of social justice and economic benefits. These are rights that belong to us as citizens.

But some of you will argue that there are real dangers
for social policy from a return to biological thinking in
psychology.

I personally see no necessary connections between scientific results and any particular social policy. Science is
not politics, nor are social policies primarily dependent on
scientific evidence, however much we might wish sometimes
that they were. Policy matters depend mostly on values, and
in this society, many groups compete over the translation
of their values into policies.

Frankly, I think such pluralism is healthy, because we
as scientists have no special wisdom in policy matters. Our
unique gift to the society is the most objective look we can
manage at the nature of the human condition. We hope that information will be noticed and used to improve human lives. As
citizens, we can try to be heard, so that our work will have
the effects we personally value, but in doing so we must be
very careful not to throw away our unique contribution--a
set of methods and standards of truthfulness that distinguish
us from many other groups.

In sum, I do not regret psychology's swing toward biology, if the excesses I cited can be avoided. A look at the
wisdom of the past will help us avoid that extreme.

References

1. A.M. Clarke and A.D.B. Clarke, Early Experience : Myth and Evidence (New York: Free Press, 1976).
2. M. Cole,J.Gay, J.Glick, and D.Sharp, The Cultural Context of Learning and Thinking (New York: Basic Books,1971).
3. A. Davis and J. Dollard, Caste and Class in a Southern Town (London: Oxford University, H. Milford Press,1937.
4. T. Dobzhansky, Genetic Diversity and Human Equality (New York : Basic Books, 1973).
5. T. Dobzhansky, Mankind Evolving : The Evolution of the Human Species ,(New Haven : Yale University Press,1962).
6. I.I. Gottesman, Genetic Aspects of Intelligent Behavior, in Handbook of Mental Deficiency, N. Ellis, ed.(New York: McGraw-Hill, 1963, pp253-296.
7. J. Hirsch, Jensenism: The Bankruptcy of "Science" Without Scholarship; Educational Theory 25, 1975, pp 3-27.
8. A.R. Jensen, Cumulative Deficit in IQ of Blacks in the Rural South; Developmental Psychology 13, 1977, pp 184-191.
9. E.H. Lenneberg, Biological Foundations of Language (New York: John Wiley and Sons,Inc.,1967).
10. E. Mayr, American Scientist,62 (2),1974,pp 650-665.
11. E. Mayr, Populations, Species,and Evolution, (Cambridge: Harvard Univ. Press, 1970).
12. F.B. Palmer, Has Compensatory Education Failed ? (mimeo), 1977
13. S. Scarr, Genetic Effects on Human Behavior: Recent Family Studies. A Master Lecture, delivered at the annual meeting of the American Psychological Association, San Francisco, Aug. 26,1977.
14. S. Scarr-Salapatek, Science, 1971a, 174 ,pp 1285-1295.
15. S. Scarr-Salapatek, Science, 1971b, 174 ,pp 1223-1228
16. S. Scarr-Salapatek, in Origins of Intelligence: Infancy and Early Childhood , M. Lewis,ed. (New York: Plenum, 1978), pp165-197.
17. S. Scarr and R.A. Weinberg, American Psychologist, 1976, 31 , pp 726-739.
18. S. Scarr,A.J.Pakstis, S.H.Katz, and W.B.Barker, Human Genetics, 1977, 857, pp 1-18.
19. S. Scarr and R.A. Weinberg. Intelligence, 1977, 1(2), pp 170-191.
20. K. Shuttleworth, Journal of Educational Psychology, 1935, 26, pp 655-681.
21. R.S. Woodworth, Heredity and Environment, (New York : Social Science Research Council, 1941).
22. E. Zigler, Effectiveness of Headstart : Another Look. Invited Address, Divisions 7 and 15, annual meeting of the American Psychological Association, San Francisco, August 27, 1977.

5. Biocultural Interactions and Sociobiology

A new "dirty" word has recently emerged in western science. Emotional diatribes previously directed toward proponents of eugenics (and to a lesser extent toward behavioral geneticists) have a new target--sociobiology. Scholarly journals, the popular press, and the political forum all provide examples of negative reactions to the tenets and implications of sociobiology that range from skeptical to condemnatory. Biological bases for behavior are often acceptable for non-human organisms, but when sociobiological principles are extrapolated to humans, humans become wary. At stake are questions that have vexed scientists, philosophers, and humanists for centuries. Are we unique? Do we differ qualitatively from all other creatures in our intellectual capabilities? Are mind, soul, free-will, language, self-consciousness, and culture properties of our species alone? Will we soon be able to modify our environment according to rational (or irrational) precepts with the result that we can control our evolutionary trajectory as well as the rate of change along this trajectory?

E. O. Wilson (1978) contends that human nature can be studied empirically using the methodology of scientific materialism. He also proposes that this naturalistic view of human nature leads to three great spiritual dilemmas: (1) that no species has a purpose beyond the imperatives created by its genetic history, (2) that conscious choices must be made among our innate mental propensities, and (3) that the human species has the capability to change its own nature. Wilson's work has engendered yet another round of nature-nuture polemics. It seems to me that the great paradox inherent in Wilson's expressed view of human nature is that although the capacity for culture has biological roots, humans have been programmed to free themselves from the constraints of their genetic programming. This does not deny the biological bases of behavior in terms of genetic influen-

ces on neural structure and function, especially during ontogeny. It merely stresses that the leash held by our genes
is quite long, indeed, and permits many degrees of freedom in
expressed behavior.

The maxim that the phenotype results from a complex interaction between the genotype and the environment has not
been especially productive in elucidating how these components actually interact to produce the observable characteristics of a human being. Decades of twin studies, heritability estimates, and attempts to delimit reaction norms have
been beset by methodological, statistical, and interpretive
difficulties. The basic assumption that sociobiology makes
is that there is a biological basis for social behavior.
Specifically, it assumes that all phenotypes (including be-
haviors--the psychophenes of behavioral genetics) at every
stage of ontogeny result from this genotype-environment interaction. While this may be true, we still don't know how
it actually occurs.

Barash (1977) formulates what he believes is the basic
assumption of sociobiology in a very different manner in an
attempt to operationalize the study of the biological bases
of behavior. His formulation is called the Central Theorem
of Sociobiology which states that insofar as the behavior in
question is genetically influenced, animals ought to behave
so as to maximize their inclusive fitness. Inclusive fitness is defined as the sum of individual fitness and genetic
representation through relatives. The concept thus includes
both individual Darwinian fitness and the effects of kin
selection. Sociobiology provides a challenge to neo-
Darwinian evolutionary theory. For our species it entails
the application of a biologically-based paradigm to realms of
inquiry previously considered to be the province of the
social sciences.

It has been more than a century since Darwin published
The Descent of Man and Selection in Relation to Sex, wherein
he unambiguously stated that humans are animals and subject
to the same evolutionary processes as other organisms. Sociobiologists content that natural selection is of paramount
importance for the explanation of the evolution of behavioral
patterns. This amounts to extending the application of
natural selection as the explanatory paradigm of genetic and
morphological change to the realm of behavior. In so doing
there has been a neglect of stochastic evolutionary processes
while making natural selection a monolithic explanatory focus.
The dynamics of inter- and intra-population behavioral transmission have also been underemphasized. Human behavior can
be studied within the framework of evolutionary theory but

sociobiologists must become more synthetic in their approach. The first step should be the construction of reasonable models of cultural inheritance. Promising developments in this direction include the efforts of Morton and Rao (1978) based on Wright's (1921) seminal paper, the work of Cavalli-Sforza and Feldman (1973), and the paper in this volume by Richerson and Boyd.

Wilson severely underestimated academic territoriality when (in his more exuberant moments) he threatened to sub-sume the subject matter of much of the social sciences under the flag of sociobiology. However, he did provide a valu-able service in his 1975 book, Sociobiology: The New Synthesis, by drawing attention to the fact that ethologists, comparative psychologists, primatologists, human biologists, neurophysiologists, ecologists, population biologists, evo-lutionary biologists, sociologists, political scientists, economists, philosophers, historians, and anthropologists do have much to offer each other. Frequently they were asking the same sorts of questions without realizing their kinship to other disciplines. Unfortunately, the prospect for a unified behavioral science seems premature given the fac-tionalism within many of the aforementioned disciplines (let alone between them). To take one example, anthropology is currently divided into cultural anthropology, physical (biological) anthropology, archaeology, and linguistics, and the commonalities in theory and method among these subdisci-plines are few.

The two central concerns of physical anthropology are the study of human origins and human variation. During the last two decades the amount of data available for the study of these two topics has increased enormously. East African deposits have yielded dozens of hominid fossils since 1959 that have changed our entire perspective on human evolution. Electrophoresis has likewise opened up another Pandora's box, the study of genetic variation within and between human populations. Protein polymorphisms are more abundant than the classical theory of population genetics and genetic load calculations would have led us to believe. Our species is characterized by its adaptability. Superimposed on our genetic variability (which differs little from that of other mammals) is our enormous capacity for behavioral adjustment to environmental demands. Our species has the potential to continue evolving both biologically and culturally. The important questions for our future involve to what extent will our cultural evolution be non-genetic or, conversely, to what extent will biological predispositions limit or influence culture change. Once again, we have no answers and there is an acrimonious difference of opinion among

scientists who are trying to unravel the complexities of
human nature.

Biocultural Interactions

I believe that a potentially significant line of research for understanding the biological bases of behavior
involves the documentation and explanation of biocultural
interactions. Whether these studies are considered to be
"sociobiological" is immaterial. For instance, primary
adult lactase deficiency has been studied extensively
(Harrison 1975; McCracken 1970, 1971; Simoons 1969, 1970,
1973). Both McCracken (1971) and Simoons (1970, 1973) believe that racial differences in this trait are due to genetic adaptations of populations in response to the practice
of dairying and consumption of milk in lactose-rich forms by
adults (Harrison 1975). These authors point to a direct influence of culture on biology. Bayless (1971, 1972) argues
that causality flows in the opposite direction. Specifically, Bayless (1971) believes that genetic drift or selection for another trait resulted in populations with high
lactase sufficiency prevalences which, in turn, developed
dairying because of their ability to consume milk.
Harrison's (1975) review article concludes that the western
pattern of lactase sufficiency developed from the practice
of drinking milk and thus culture has affected biology and
not vice-versa. The world-wide distribution of lactose
tolerance seems to be consistent with a selectionist explanation in milking populations; however, the exact mechanism
of selection is still unknown. Two different hypotheses
have been put forth regarding the actual selective mechanism.
McCracken (1971) and Simoons (1970) both favor the idea that
adult milk consumption conferred a non-specific nutritional
advantage in certain environments that was reflected in differential reporduction. Flatz and Rotthauwe (1973) are more
specific by proposing that since lactose facilitates the
intestinal absorption of calcium, lactase sufficiency could
counteract the effects of vitamin D deficiency and would
confer a selective advantage in northern European climates.
Harrison (1975) concurs with Flatz and Rotthauwe (1973) in
that their hypothesis of a selective advantage based on the
role of lactose in facilitating calcium absorption makes
sense in terms of mammaliam evolution (since mammaliam milk
supplies both lactose and calcium).

The exact genetic basis for adult lactase deficiency is
still unknown. Much of the early work pointed to an anto-
somal recessive inheritance mechanism for lactase deficiency.
According to Ferguson and Maxwell (1967), the trait is controlled at a single autosomal locus with three alleles:

L (dominant) l_1 (recessive), and l_2 (recessive). The L-geno-
type results in the lactose tolerant phenotype. The l_1l_1
homozygote results in primary adult lactase deficiency and
the l_2l_2 homozygote results in the rare condition known as
congenital alactasia. Subsequent work by Gilat and others
(1973) suggests that alteration of a regulatory gene may be
involved. Harrison (1975) also entertains the possibility
that multiple-threshold models may be applicable to data on
lactose tolerance and might be helpful to distinguish between
single-gene and multifactorial inheritance for this trait.

The lactase example highlights attempts to unravel biocultural interactions. Humans cannot escape the fact that
they must eat to satisfy their energy requirements as biological entities. Cultural food-getting behavior provides a
possible line of attack for sociobiologists as well as for
other investigators interested in the interaction of biology
and culture in human populations. We certainly have biological limitations for our dietary. There are eight diet-
dependent amino acids essential for our metabolic maintenance (nine for growing children who also require histidine)
and we must have a balanced intake of these essential nutrients within a twenty-four hour period for effective utilization. Balanced diets include more than just protein, the
source of amino acids. Carbohydrates, fats, vitamins, and
minerals are all needed in certain quantities to ensure
metabolic efficiency. As the nutritional biochemist Harold
Draper (1978) has cogently pointed out, there are no essential foods but there are essential nutrients. Whether one
gets the essential amino acids from meat or from a mixed
vegetarian diet of corn, beans, and squash is unimportnat.
What is important is that a person is not mal- or under-
nourished; that essential nutrients are not lacking in the
dietary.

The rapidly changing Eskimo dietary provides another
potentially rewarding focus for understanding the interplay
of biology and culture. The aboriginal diet of the Eskimos
who lived north of the Arctic Circle consisted almost entirely of meat and fish. Draper (1978) concludes that
despite its lack of variety this diet was capable of fur-
nishing all the nutrients essential for nutritional health
provided adequate amounts were available and traditional
food preparation techniques were observed. In view of the
high-protein, low-carbohydrate dietary of these people the
central problem in adaptational bioenergetics for the
Eskimo was the maintenance of glucose homeostasis. The
brain needs glucose to survive and function. If no carbohydrate glucose source is available, alternative strategies
are necessary for survival. Glucose cannot be synthesized

from fatty acids. Draper (1978) believes that homeostasis was maintained primarily by glucose synthesis from dietary amino acids. Hence, a high protein diet was a necessary feature of the aboriginal Eskimo diet. Both protein synthesis and glucose synthesis depended on dietary amino acids (Zegura and Jamison 1978).

While meat is high in protein it is noticeably low in calcium content. The aboriginal Eskimo dietary included little calcium. Dairy products were scarce. Only soft bones of fish and the spongy portion of land and sea mammal bones yielded appreciable amounts of this essential mineral. Draper (1978) postulates that the Eskimo possess a vitamin-D-dependent mechanism which enables the body to adapt to varying calcium intakes by modifying absorption efficiency. The unique metabolic capabilities of the Eskimo are also reflected in their body fat composition. Dietary rather than biosynthetic fatty acids consittuted the bulk of their body fat. Lack of excess dietary glucose and an excess of dietary fatty acids combined to inhibit lipogenesis with the result that long-chain polyunsaturated fatty acids typical of marine mammal oils were prevalent in Eskimo adipose tissue. This relatively large proportion of polyunsaturated fats in native foods (unlike the high saturated fatty acid content usually ascribed to animal fats) may have contributed to the low serum cholesterol levels of Eskimos in previous generations (Zegura and Jamison 1978).

Acculturation has caused a rapid disappearance of the aboriginal Eskimo diet. The discovery of oil, the signing of the Native Claims Bill in 1971, and increased contact with non-Eskimo values and behavior patterns have eroded the traditional way of life of the Eskimo. Processed foods high in carbohydrate content have become widely available. Some essential nutrients are now in short supply while others are present in excess. The metabolic consequences of these dietary changes are as yet unclear; however, some alarming trends are already evident. The most significant effect of the change to a modern dietary has been the sharp increase in dental caries documented by Dahlberg and others (1978). Obesity has also become a significant problem for adult Eskimo women (Colbert and others 1978). Bone loss occurs at a relatively early age in Eskimos and the rate of bone loss is accelerated compared with other human populations (Mazess and Mather 1978). High protein (and therefore phosphorus) intake coupled with low calcium and vitamin D availability in the aboriginal diet may be contributory to this observed pattern of extensive bone loss but the exact causation remains unclear (Zegura and Jamison 1978). The traditional Eskimo profile of low blood cholesterol, low blood pressure,

and lean body mass no longer obtains for many Eskimo populations. The interaction of changing diet, obesity, hyperten-
sion, hypercholesterolemia, cardiovascular disease, and
atherosclerosis remains a potentially rewarding area of
future research among modern Eskimo populations (Zegura and
Jamison 1978).

Bell and others (1978) performed lactose tolerance tests
in Wainwright and Point Hope, Alaska, and found a limited
capacity for lactose digestion as would be expected since
these Eskimos lack a history of dairying. More interesting
was their finding of sucrose intolerance, confirmed in six
individuals on the basis of oral load tests. At present
this form of familial sucrose intolerance seems to be unique
to Eskimo populations, having been found only in Greenland
and Alaskan Eskimos. The degree of intolerance to sucrose
seems to be more acute than for lactose. In addition,
sucrose deficiency is not confined to adults and older
children, as in the case of lactase deficiency. Sucrose
intolerance represents a potential problem for both Eskimo
adults and children. The modern influx of processed foods
makes it increasingly difficult to avoid sucrose in the diet.
In the arctic region sucrose was virtually absent in the
aboriginal dietary and lack of intestinal sucrose was probably not harmful. Now, however, a class of proprietary
foods may have to be developed for sucrose-intolerant individuals (Zegura and Jamison 1978).

The topic of biocultural interaction will continue to
be studied by cultural anthropologists, physical anthropologists, human biologists, and human ecologists whether the
emerging discipline of sociobiology becomes established or
not. Sociobiology stresses disciplinary unification; a
truly synthetic science of behavior based on biological
principles. Only future developments in method and theory
can justify the inclusion of biocultural research under the
rubric "sociobiology." It is my belief that many years of
analysis lie ahead before a productive synthesis will emerge.

References

Barash, D.P. 1977 Sociobiology and Behavior. New York:
    Elsevier.
Bayless, T.M. 1971 "Junior, why didn't you drink your
    milk?" Gastroenterology 60:479-480. _____
    _____ 1972 "Lactose intolerance and dietary
    evolution." Gastroenterology 63:524-525.
Bell, R.R., H.H. Draper, and J.G. Bergan. 1978. "Metabolic
    parameters: lactose and sucrose tolerance," in Eskimos
    of Northwestern Alaska: A Biological Perspective, P.L.

Jamison, S.L. Zegura, and F.A. Milan (eds.), Stroudsburg: Dowden, Hutchinson and Ross. Pp. 184-188.

Colbert, M.J., G.V. Mann, and L.M. Hursh. 1978 "Nutritional studies: clinical observations on nutritional
health," in Eskimos of Northwestern Alaska: A Biological Perspective, P.L. Jamison, S.L. Zegura, and F.A.
Milan (Eds.), Stroudsburg: Dowden, Hutchinson and Ross.
Pp. 162-173.

Cavalli-Sforza, L.L., and M.W. Feldman. 1973 "Models for
cultural inheritance: I. group mean and within group
variation." Theoretical Population Biology 4:42-55.

Dahlberg, A.A., R. Cederquist, J. Mayhall, and D. Owen.
1978 "Eskimo craniofacial studies," in Eskimos of
Northwestern Alaska: A Biological Perspective, P.L.
Jamison, S.L. Zegura, and F.A. Milan (Eds.), Stroudsberg: Dowden, Hutchinson and Ross. Pp. 94-113.

Darwin, C. 1871 The Descent of Man and Selection in Relation to Sex. London: Murray.

Draper, H.H. 1978 "Nutritional studies: the aboriginal
Eskimo diet--a modern perspective," in Eskimos of
Northwestern Alaska: A Biological Perspective, P.L.
Jamison, S.L. Zegura, and F.A. Milan (Eds.),
Stroudsberg: Dowden, Hutchinson and Ross. Pp. 139-144.

Flatz, G., and H.W. Rotthauwe. 1973 "Lactose nutrition
and natural selection." Lancet 2:76-77.

Ferguson, A., and J.D. Maxwell. 1967 "Genetic aetiology
of lactose intolerance." Lancet 2:188-190.

Gilat, T., Y. Benaroya, E. Gelman-Malachi, and A. Adam. 1973
"Genetics of primary adult lactase deficiency."
Gastroenterology 64:562-568.

Harrison, G.G. 1975 "Primary adult lactase deficiency: a
problem in anthropological genetics." American
Anthropologist 77:812-835.

Mazess, R.B., and W. Mather. 1978 "Biochemical variation:
bone mineral content," in Eskimos of Northwestern
Alaska: A Biological Perspective, P.L. Jamison, S.L.
Zegura, and F.A. Milan (Eds.), Stroudsberg: Dowden,
Hutchinson and Ross. Pp. 134-138.

McCracken, R.D. 1970 "Adult lactose intolerance." Journal
of the American Medical Association 213:2257-2260.

_____ 1971 "Lactase deficiency: an example of
dietary evolution." Current Anthropology 12:479-517.

Morton, N.E., and D.C. Rao. 1978 "Quantitative inheritance in man." Yearbook of Physical Anthropology 21:
12-41.

Simoons, F.J. 1969 "Primary adult lactose intolerance and
the milking habit: a problem in biological and cultural
interrelations. I. Review of the medical research."
American Journal of Digestive Diseases 14:819-836.

_____ 1970 "Primary adult lactose intolerance and the milking habit: a problem in biological and cultural interrelations. II. A culture historical hypothesis." American Journal of Digestive Diseases 15:695-710.

_____ 1973 "Progress report. New light on ethnic differences in adult lactose intolerance." American Journal of Digestive Diseases 18:595-611.

Wilson, E.O. 1975 Sociobiology: The New Synthesis. Cambridge: Harvard University Press.

_____ 1978 On Human Nature. Cambridge: Harvard University Press.

Wright, S. 1921 "Systems of Mating." Genetics 6:111-178.

Zegura, S.L., and P.L. Jamison. 1978 "Multidisciplinary research: a case study in Eskimo human biology," in Eskimos of Northwestern Alaska: A Biological Perspective, P.L. Jamison, S.L. Zegura, and F.A. Milan (Eds.), Stroudsburg: Dowden, Hutchinson and Ross. Pp. 262-287.

6. Culture, Biology and the Evolution of Variation Between Human Groups

"The American aborigines, Negroes, and Europeans
are as different from each other in mind as any three
races that can be named; yet I was incessantly struck,
while living with the Fuegians on board the 'Beagle,'
with the many little traits of character showing how
similar their minds were to ours; and so it was with a
full-blooded negro with whom I happened once to be
intimate."

> Charles Darwin
> The Descent of Man and
> Selection in Relation to Sex,
> 2nd Edition, p. 237 (1874)

Abstract

Understanding the variation of human behavior in
scientific terms requires an explicit mechanistic account of
the influence of genes and culture on human phenotypes.
In this paper we construct a model of the evolutionary
process in humans by assuming that culture is a system of
inheritance evolving in parallel with the genetic system.
The special properties of the cultural system and its linkage
to the genetic system are specified in enough detail to make
possible a simple, but reasonably complete and realistic,
theoretical analysis of the problem. The central conclusion
of this analysis is that, given the known properties of
culture and its presumed evolutionary advantages, it is
implausible that human behavior can be predicted entirely by
considerations of genetic fitness. So long as a cultural
system is any genetic advantage at all, a structural
constraint is imposed on genetic fitness optimization. A
genetically optimal capacity for culture will cause cultural
fitness to have an effect on phenotype as well. The magnitude
of the cultural fitness effect depends on the degree to which
the processes of cultural evolution can be constrained by the

organic capacity for culture without sacrificing the benefits
of the cultural mode of adaptation. Determining the nature
of this tradeoff is an empirical problem. The evidence for
humans suggests our species' behavioral variation is caused
by cultural processes controlled by powerful but rather simple
and general genetic constraints.

Introduction

One of the most striking and unusual features of the
human species is the great diversity of adaptive strategies
we exhibit. Providing a place for this and other puzzling
anomalies of the human case in the Darwinian theory of
organic evolution has proven to be a difficult and controversial task. The central difficulty has been lack of
agreement about the role of culture in human evolution. The
purpose of this paper is to show one way that humans can be
incorporated into that theory without being trapped within a
"cyclical and repetitive opposition" of ideas about natural
and cultural influences on our behavior (1). We will begin
by sketching the fundamental weaknesses of the various positions in the nature-nurture controversy. Then, the central
part of the paper describes a rudimentary model of the co-
evolution of genes and culture that is designed to capture
the basic features of human evolution, with a more formal
account of the model given in an appendix. Finally, we will
examine some of the broad features of the human species in
the light of this model. We will devote special attention
to the question of the basis of the similarities and differences between human groups. We believe that it is in the
structure of the capacity for culture and in the resulting
interplay between the cultural and genetic systems of inheritance that we shall find the solution to the problem
that plagued Darwin in Descent of Man (2) (see particularly
Chapter 7, "On the races of man") of how such major differences in human behavior could exist despite the trivial
nature of the organic differences between humans. In particular we will argue that a genetic capacity for culture
arose in substantial part because it made the evolution of
major group differences possible. It is difficult for major
genetic differences to arise within an interbreeding species
unless selection is quite strong, because gene flow so effectively reduces between group differences. The properties
of cultural inheritance can greatly facilitate the evolution
of between group cultural differences. Our final conclusion
is that the evidence is consistent with the hypothesis that
genetic effects on behavior are strong but simple and universal, and that the details of behavior by which groups differ are the result of cultural evolution guided by the
genetic universals.

Review of the Problem

Progress on the nature-nurture problem since 1874 has been modest. Although no modern school of scholarly opinion doubts that humans evolved from some hominoid ape in the last few million years, the character of the evolutionary processes that have prevailed in this time period and that presently prevail are still extremely controversial. The fundamental question in this controversy is how the cultural inheritance of phenotype affects evolutionary dynamics. Again, no school of opinion questions the idea that a massive capacity for culture is the chief distinguishing feature of the human species or that one of the main problems of human evolution is how this capacity increased from modest beginnings, comparable to the protocultural transmission in modern apes, to the present spectacular capacities for symbolic codification and artifact production that characterize Homo sapiens. Beyond these obvious rudiments, agreement disappears. How did the capacity for culture arise? How do cultural and genetic inheritance interact? What are the adaptive advantages and disadvantages of a cultural capacity? Its advantages of flexibility and speed are easy to imagine, yet only humans have much capacity for culture despite widespread protocultural preadaptations. Why then is culture capacity so rare?

The contemporary sociobiology controversy illustrates the insecure grasp we still have on the answers to such questions a century after the publication of Descent. Opinions tend to polarize at the extremes of possible hypotheses. On the one hand, some biologists and social scientists hold "all genes" hypotheses, proposing that genes control much of human social behavior directly (3), or that by some other means, considerations of individual (inclusive) genetic fitness are sufficient to predict the details of human behavior, culture notwithstanding (4). The increasing sophistication of evolutionary interpretations of animal social behavior, as documented in E. O. Wilson's Sociobiology (5) has lent an air of plausibility to these hypotheses by emphasizing the continuum of mental capacities and behaviors which link humans to other animals, particularly to the higher primates. E. O. Wilson (6) is, nevertheless, himself not a proponent of a simple "all genes" hypothesis.

On the other hand, in reaction to the renewed interest in "all genes" hypotheses, an explicit defense of an "all culture" hypothesis has been given. Marshall Sahlins (7) has developed the most extensive such hypothesis in the context of the contemporary debate. He tries to show that human cultures evolve by a mechanism of cultural logic utterly

different from natural selection and almost completely free
from biological imperatives.

Many scientists have eschewed polar views as empirically
unreasonable and instead have held a more syncretic position.
Theodosius Dobzhansky (8), in his influential book Mankind
Evolving and in numerous articles on the subject, was the
most prominent and prolific spokesman for the position that
both genes and culture interact reciprocally in a unified
evolutionary process. Many social scientists have also
stressed that the cultural system, whatever its own peculiar
properties, is intimately linked to social organization,
ecological settings and biological processes (9).

The aim here is not to review this controversy. However,
we wish to argue that the extreme views, as usually espoused,
are logically or empirically faulty and that, although the
syncretic position is too vague on essential points to constitute a complete theory, it is essentially correct.

A satisfactory theory of human evolution requires, at
the minimum, three elements. First, it requires an evolutionary process for the genetic system; second, an evolutionary process for the cultural system and third, some way
of relating the two systems through their joint effect on
phenotype. Given a specification of the state of the genetic
system, the cultural system and the environment at a given
time, the theory must predict, (although at the outset only
in principle) the state of the cultural and genetic systems
at some future time of interest. Richard Lewontin (10) has
termed theories which satisfy these minimal criteria "dynamically sufficient." A useful theory should also have
empirical referents and should be capable of explaining the
circumstances which permit culture to arise and the conditions under which it might transcend biology. The theory
must be consistent with the presently accepted findings of
the human and biological sciences and should generate hypotheses falsifiable by future investigation. Anatol
Rapoport (11) argues that the scientific resolution of apparent paradoxes like the nature-nurture problem have
typically been accomplished by reformulating them in terms
of linkage and continuum. Therefore, we might expect that
a successful theory will reduce to the extreme hypotheses
in the limit and offer a means of empirical resolution of
the question of just where a particular organism, say contemporary humans, lies on the continuum.

The fundamental difficulty with "all genes" hypotheses
is that they take no account of the fact that culture constitutes a second system of inheritance. The simple concept

of individual fitness cannot be entirely appropriate for an
organism that receives information determining phenotype from
two sources. Cultural inheritance is something like an extra
chromosome, but a chromosome whose mechanics of inheritance
differ from genes. Human evolution is a problem in the co-
evolution of two systems of inheritance and this fact must
have at least some interesting consequences. Thus "all
genes" hypotheses violate Lewontin's criterion of dynamic
sufficiency by failing to incorporate the known properties of
the cultural system.

The most obvious difficulty with "all culture" hypotheses is origins. Although it may very well turn out to
be true that contemporary humans have transcended natural
selection, a bald culturogenic hypothesis gives us no idea
about how transcendence might have occurred. This lack would
not be completely damaging if culturogenic theories had a
clear mechanism for the control of genetic variation by cultural processes. But Sahlin's argument, at least, is based
on a claim of extreme ecological possibilism we find quite
unconvincing (12). Given that Neo-Darwinism is an acceptable
mechanistic theory explaining the evolutionary process for
ordinary organisms, a complete account of human transcendence
must ultimately be able to give a mechanistic description of
the origin process. Thus, an "all culture" hypothesis also
fails the test of dynamic sufficiency.

The inadequacy of Dobzhansky's (8) position is rather
more subtle and less severe. In <u>Mankind Evolving</u> and in his
other writings on the subject, he disparages both extreme
views. For Dobzhansky, cultural and genetic processes are
interrelated, interdependent, and linked by feedback. The
capacity for culture is clearly a genetically coded adap-
tion, but just as clearly exercises no specific control on
the culture acquired. The problem is that these reasonable
propositions are also not quite a dynamically sufficient
theory of the evolution of an organism with two systems of
inheritance. They are so general that any result from "all
genes" to "all culture" is possible, and Dobzhansky gives no
testable proposition or measurable parameter to use to decide the case. This problem is clearly evident in <u>Mankind
Evolving</u>. Within the space of a single page (p. 20),
Dobzhansky first asserts that "the interrelations between
the biological and cultural components of human evolution
may be brought out most clearly if we consider that they
serve the same basic function -- adaptation to and control of
man's environment." This statement standing alone, and
assuming that Dobzhansky means "adaptation" in the usual
Darwinian sense, sounds very much like an "all genes" hypothesis. However, after briefly recounting the biological

basis of the capacity for culture and the adaptive advantages
of culture, he writes "... in producing the genetic basis of
culture, biological evolution has transcended itself -- it
has produced the superorganic." The most obvious interpretation of this statement is an "all culture" hypothesis.
Dobzhansky goes on to say that the "superorganic has not
annulled the organic" which could mean almost anything from
actual control of genetic evolution by cultural processes
through environmental manipulation, to some compromise between the cultural and genetic processes. Thus, although
quite reasonable as far as it goes, Dobzhansky's approach
does not offer a mechanistic analysis of the problem which
can distinguish between the extremes of the present debate.
Nor does it give a clear picture of how human phenotypes
might have passed from Darwinian adaptations to superorganic
transcendence in the course of evolution.

E. O. Wilson's (6) recent discussions of the culture-
genes problem are rather similar to Dobzhansky's, and both,
in contrast to some sociobiologists, view it as a sort of
coevolutionary phenomenon in which both systems play important roles in human evolution. Dual inheritance models
are simply a formalization (and an elaboration) of this
intuitively reasonable position. Our claim is that making
Dobzhansky's and Wilson's ideas more concrete by adding a
few additional postulates results in a quite plausible
dynamically sufficient theory.

Definitions and Assumptions

First, we will assume that the properties of the genetic
system are those conventionally given in population genetics
and evolutionary biology. In particular, we will make the
usual, if over-simplified, assumption that natural selection
acting on genotype tends to optimize individual fitness (13).
No such conventional or well understood assumption can be
made for the cultural system. Rather, we will make and defend more controversial and problematic postulates.

Before outlining these postulates, it is important to
clearly distinguish culturally inherited traits as those
passed from individual to individual, either by teaching or
imitation, and thus from generation to generation. The more
general category of learned traits includes knowledge that
is learned de novo by each individual. This distinction is
important. In order to predict the state of the cultural
system (e.g. the values of cultural quantities analogous to
gene frequencies), one must know the state of the cultural
system at previous times. Culture is distinguished from
ordinary trial-and-error learning by the existence of

tradition. Thus the state of the cultural system is endogenous to the system, and a dynamically sufficient model must
include a model of the dynamics of cultural processes. In
contrast, de novo learned behavior is merely an elaborate
form of phenotypic plasticity -- and can thus be explained
by conventional Neo-Darwinian interaction of an endogenous
genetic system and an exogenous environment.

We first assume that since cultural effects persist
longer than an individual's lifetime and affect behavior in
important ways, they constitute an inheritance system.
Several recent discussions of the evidence from experimental
psychology and psychological anthropology have interpreted
culture in a way that is consistent with this assumption
(14). The lengthy review of experimental evidence for social
learning by Ted Rosenthal and Barry Zimmerman is particularly
convincing. They summarize a large body of evidence that
indicates that children are particularly adept at acquiring
rules and conceptual principles from adult models, even in
the absence of direct reinforcement. They call attention
to the stability of behavior acquired by social learning
(due to accurate copying of the rule or skill) and to the
variation among individuals of the products of social learning (due to exposure to different models).

The problem of determining the sources of variation in
human I.Q. provides an excellent example of the reasonable-
ness of the cultural inheritance assumption. I.Q. has very
high measured heritability, a fact which led some observers
(15) to conclude that this heritability had a genetic basis.
However, it is clear from theoretical considerations (16)
that if variation in I.Q. is even partly a result of cultural
factors, then the effects of children initating parents and
learning skills from them will be rather thoroughly con-
founded with genetic effects. If adoption agencies frequently place children in families similar to those of the
natural parents, and if adults generally model for children
"appropriate" racial, ethnic and class behavior, even
identical twins raised apart will have a cultural component
to the measured heritability of traits such as I.Q. The
empirical investigations of Sandra Scarr (17) show just how
difficult it is to separate genetic, cultural and simple
environmental influences on such a trait. The important
point for our discussion is that behaviors learned by the
cultural mechanisms by children from their natural parents
can mimic genetic determination almost exactly, so far as
easily observed differences in phenotype are concerned. We
will shortly give examples of situations where the differences between the two systems are likely to be apparent, but
let us pursue the limiting case of very great similarity to

its obvious conclusion: Cultural inheritance will frequently
produce effects on the behavior of individuals that are highly correlated with any genetic markers that may exist, even
if the genetic markers are themselves trivial.

Darwin's analysis of the problem of the differences between human races deserves to be better appreciated than it
is on this point (2). On the basis of a careful survey of
the then extant evidence on racial differences, Darwin concluded that main observable organic differences between races
were due to the effects of sexual selection. That is why his
most extensive discussion of sexual selection is paired with
his most extensive discussion of the human species in
Descent. The organic similarities of the races with regard
to ordinary adaptive traits appeared so thoroughgoing,
Darwin was led to attribute their differences in "mind" to
the effects of "inherited habit." Dual inheritance theory
can be read as the extension and formalization of this conclusion in the light of the modern discovery that genes determine organic structures, and the differences between
human minds are chiefly cultural.

The second postulate regarding culture is that because
it is a system of inheritance, it will be subject to evolutionary processes that resemble the evolutionary processes
acting on the genetic system: The cultural system will exhibit analogs of mutation, recombination and selection.
Donald Campbell (18) has given a very clear deductive argument along these lines. If culture is inherited, if it is
variable between individuals, and if it affects individual
competence in a given environment, some cultural variants
will be more likely to pass their culture to individuals of
the next generation than others. In other words, we assume
that humans, like other organisms, compete in particular
ecological situations for scarce resources and that behaviors
acquired culturally are crucial in this competition. Hence,
the differential "reproduction" of cultural variants is as
important to human evolution as the reproduction of genetic
variants, perhaps more important. Campbell's argument is
just that, at this level of generality, the Darwinian logic
of natural selection is as valid for culture as it is for
genes. Several other authors have also suggested that culture
is subject to natural selection (19).

I.Q. may provide an example of a culturally inherited
trait that has been modified by selection. Carl Bajema (20)
investigated the completed family size, as a function of
I.Q., of a cohort of school children administered an I.Q.
test by the Kalamazoo school system in 1916-17. He discovered that the mean family size of persons with lower than

normal I.Q. (the class midpoint in his study was 74) was
smaller than for higher I.Q. classes, largely because many
lower I.Q. individuals failed to form families. If we assume
that the skills in abstract reasoning that I.Q. measures,
are acquired largely by the cultural mechanism and that such
skills are important for coping with life in modern industrial societies, then Bajema has approximated a measurement
of selection acting on a cultural trait. This interpretation
is reminicent of Claude Levi-Strauss' (21) ideas about minds.
He suggests that modern western peoples are characterized by
their preoccupation with the abstract while in general, non-
western peoples are characterized by a more concrete and
particular appreciation of their worlds. It is easy to imagine, we think, that such differences could have arisen
gradually by the differential "reproduction" of cultural
variants.

Postulating that culturally determined traits are subject to selective retention, leaves several important questions to be answered. What is the unit of selection: the
individual, the cultural trait, perhaps the group? This
question has been posed quite explicitly by Ted Cloak (22).
How is variability maintained? Are frequency-dependent or
interspecies effects dominant? The analysis of these questions entails the construction of explicit, dynamic models
similar to the type in common use in population genetics. A
very useful beginning on models of this type has been developed by Marcus Feldman and L. L. Cavalli-Sforza (23).
Such models require assumptions about the details of the
system of inheritance but there is, unfortunately, no general agreement on the details of cultural inheritance. This
fact, however, is not fatal. For a variety of empirical and
computational reasons, many analogous questions have not been
satisfactorily answered for natural selection acting on genes
(24). Nonetheless, most biologists are comfortable with the
idea that organic evolution acts to produce adapted individuals, i.e., the organisms we observe generally are of a
phenotype that, at least approximately, maximizes individual
genetic fitness.

We suggest a similar postulate for natural selection
acting on culture: There is a quantity, called cultural fitness, that represents the relative success with which alternative cultural messages reproduce themselves. Selection
acts to maximize this cultural fitness. We make this sug-
gestion not because we believe the complex questions mentioned above are uninteresting or unimportant. Nor are the
categorically different ideas of cultural evolution of social
scientists like Marshall Sahlins without interest or merit.
Rather, a simple but explicit model is the minimum first step

required to investigate the logical necessities of the interaction between cultural and genetic inheritance systems. We
are encouraged in this approach by the success and robustness
of such adaptation arguments when they are applied to genetic
natural selection, in spite of the various well known exceptions to the general principle.

The third postulate is that the phenotypes that maximize
cultural and genetic fitness will ordinarily not be identical
because the differences between the two inheritance mechanisms will cause each to respond somewhat differently to
selection. Although the example of I.Q. shows how similar
the two effects might be for some traits, in many cases the
two kinds of fitness will differ because genetic and cultural inheritance have different "life cycles." For example,
cultural traits may be acquired from entirely unrelated individuals. Other, less extreme, differences between the life
cycles of genetic and cultural inheritance include the timing
of transmission, the possibility of differential contributions of mothers and fathers in cultural inheritance, the
serial nature of cultural inheritance, and the participation
of many individuals in the enculturation of a single child.
Clearly, the phenotype that maximizes an individual's chance
of enculturating a complex set of related and unrelated individuals is not necessarily the optimum one for producing
genetic offspring.

Ronald Pulliam (25) has given a nice illustration of the
subtlety of the dual fitness effect. It is based on the
Eskimo husband's practice of inviting male guests to have
sexual relations with his wife as an act of hospitality.
Pulliam imagines that such a practice could arise by selection on culture in the following way: Eskimo villagers live
in very small, isolated communities in which inbreeding is
quite high. The deleterious effects of inbreeding in humans
are well documented (26). If the idea of wife sharing
hospitality arises by chance on the part of a given male, any
children that result from such unions are likely to be more
vigorous on account of being outbred. If such outbred
children are more likely to survive, be more successful
hunters or be more attractive mates, and if they imitate
their father's idea of hospitable behavior, then the trait
will spread. Note that the father's genetic fitness will be
greatly reduced by the work of rearing an unrelated child as
his own, even as his cultural fitness is increased.

Two systems of inheritance create a coevolutionary
situation that will eventually result in an evolutionarily
stable equilibrium between the competing selective forces.
Selection on culture-type will increase cultural fitness, and

selection on genes will increase genetic fitness step by step until an equilibrium is reached. Our hypothesis assumes that at each step until equilibrium, selection will increase cultural fitness at the prevailing genotype and genetic fitness at the prevailing culture-type. In other words, we imagine that the human evolutionary process with dual inheritance is a blind, step-by-step, selective increase in the fitness of each code, given the value of the other. At equilibrium, any change in culture-type will reduce cultural fitness given the existing genotype and visa versa. The mathematical nature of this solution is very similar to John Maynard-Smith's (27) concept of an Evolutionary Stable Strategy (ESS). What is important here is that at equilibrium, the observed traits will not necessarily appear to be at either the genetic or the cultural optimum. This fact must have a profound influence on the course of cultural evolution and for the genetic evolution of a culture-bearing organism.

In the case of genes, several processes influence the frequency of genotypes besides natural selection, including particularly migration and mutation. However, selection is the only directional process acting to produce improved phenotypes -- it is the only optimizing process. The other evolutionary processes introduce random noise which produces (ultimately) the variability on which selection operates but not the adaptation of particular variants to given environments.

In the case of an organism with two systems of inheritance, things are not quite so simple because the two systems interact. To see the problem, first consider the cultural system in isolation. The culture of individuals will vary, and some behaviors will produce more successful individuals than others, which cultural variants being successful depending upon environmental circumstances. Although success in this context might be defined in several ways, we are only interested in success which leads to cultural "reproduction," a differential opportunity to enculturate the next generation, be admired (and hence imitated) by one's fellows, and the like. A theory of cultural evolution would ultimately require explicit rules for the actual transmission system, an account of the sources of variation and so forth, but we could hope that the central role of selection in evolution would be preserved. The most serious complexity comes because culture is carried by organisms that also have genes. The genetic system can influence the evolutionary behavior of the cultural system by adjusting the organic substratum that permits culture to exist. In other words, selection operating on genes can be expected to adjust the capacity for culture in order to minimize the costs to

genetic fitness of cultural selection acting to favor cultural "reproduction" at the expense of genetic reproduction.
There are two classes of mechanisms by which selection on the
capacity for culture can affect the structure of cultural
fitness (28). One we term "symmetry." Any potential dis-
crepancy between the cultural and genetic selection regime
is minimized to the extent that the life cycles of genetic
and cultural transmission are the same. Any component of
culture that is acquired by very young children from their
parents is much like an extra chromosome, and genetic and
cultural fitness as a function of a given trait will differ
little. I.Q. appears to exhibit high symmetry. The second
we term "bias." Genes may code for a system of psychological
pleasures, pains and satisfactions that favor some cultural
variants over others. For example, sexual pleasure may be
genetically influenced and cause people to discriminate
against celibacy, even when celibate priesthoods furnish
pastors and teachers of considerable cultural influence.
Note that bias is a separate directional and organizing force
acting on culture in concert with cultural selection. If
cultural fitness is defined as that which increases with
time, it is affected by both selection and bias.

Thus, a final general postulate is required to consider
the evolution of symmetry and bias. We assume a "capacity
for culture," that is, an ability to code and inherit
cultural messages whose behavior is characterized by a system
of symmetries and biases. Since organic adaptations related
to brain size and organization, vocal tract anatomy, and
perhaps various genetically coded behaviors are prerequisites
for culture, this complex of traits is the major way in which
the genetic and cultural systems are linked in the phenotype
of individuals. We make the rather conservative Neo-
Darwinian assumption that this capacity, i.e. the amount and
kinds of symmetry and bias, is optimized with respect to
genetic fitness. It is certainly plausible that, through
mechanisms such as sexual selection or environmental modification, selection acting on culture could affect and perhaps
determine the equilibrium amount of cultural capacity.
However, our assumption produces the simplest logically complete model and must be relevant to at least the earliest
stages of the origin process.

It is important to see that even when the capacity for
culture is genetically optimal, it is by no means clear that
genes are more fundamental or more important than culture, or
even that genes can "control" the evolutionary dynamics of
the situation. All coevolutionary situations are ambiguous
in this regard. Consider the example of plant domesticates.
Here the human farmer seems like the controlling element of

evolution of the system. However, Kent Flannery (29)
observed that the plants that became domesticates were likely
to have been those with the evolutionary flexibility to respond with increased yields under human exploitation, with
the advantage to the plant that humans acted as agents of
dispersal and to favor the domesticate in competition with
other plants. As the plant species evolve greater yield,
the human populations exploiting it grow and spread geographically. Eventually, in the case of maize, large
Amerindian populations spread the plant north and south many
degrees of latitude beyond its ancestral range. While the
plant became obligately dependent on human cultivation, the
humans became very strongly dependent on the plant. From
the plant's point of view, it successfully domesticated the
farmer, as well as vice versa.

In the case of human phenotype, both genetic and cultural inheritance are obligate requisites for a functioning
organism. Debates about whether nature or nurture is more
fundamental are nonsensical. Rather, from the genetic side,
the important question is to understand how a given capacity
for culture arose, causing a particular pattern of symmetry
and a particular set of biases. From the cultural side, it
is to understand what patterns of culture arise in given
environments among people with a given culture capacity. In
the context of this symposium, we are interested in the
special question of whether or not the great variety of
human adaptations can be due primarily to variations in
culture against a background of uniform culture capacity.

A Two-Trait, Two-Capacities Model

In this paper we will consider the effects of two kinds
of culture capacities, a quantitative and a qualitative
capacity. First, we want to investigate the results of assuming that the quantitative aspect of a culture capacity has
phenotypic costs. The capacity for culture is an organic
adaptation that must be traded off against other competences;
large brains are energetically costly, fragile, inconvenient
at birth and so forth. The model in this paper incorporates
this idea by postulating an organism with two ordinary
phenotypic traits, Physiology (P), a simple surrogate for
adaptations such as running speed, strength, food processing
abilities and so forth, and Behavior (B), a similar surrogate
for a conventional class of phenotypic traits. Physiology is
assumed to be coded only by genes, Behavior by both genes
and culture. The physiological cost of expanding the culture
capacity is a reduction in values of P possible and the
potential genetic fitness advantages stem from the enlarged
set of behavioral possibilities.

Second, we want to incorporate the effects of the qualitative aspects of the culture capacity -- bias and symmetry.
It is quite plausible that the structure of the human brain
or the behavioral organization of enculturation acts with
specificity in determining what kind of culture is learned
when. A very simple model (30) can capture some direct
genetic adaptations which affect behavior if behaviors such
as sexual lustfulness are under partial genetic control. In
that case, genetic and cultural messages would "fairly" compete to determine phenotype and the one trait, one capacity
model is a reasonable simplification. However, the genetic
influences that erect filters to the kind of cultural messages which are learned may be strong and important and
need to be modelled as explicitly as possible. William
Durham (31) has presented an hypothesis along these lines.
He maintains that because the capacity for culture arose
through natural selection that "our hominid ancestors must
have had some methods of keeping culture 'on track' of the
adaptive optima as those optima varied from place to place
and changed from time to time" (32). He describes one symmetry and two bias mechanisms by which this genetic control
might be exercised: First, because the pattern of cultural
inheritance is similar to the genetic -- parents socialize
children who must survive to socialize grandchildren --
cultural and genetic fitnesses are very similar. Second, he
argues "throughout the organic evolution of hominids there
was a persistent genetic selective advantage for a neurophysiology which rewarded with sensory reinforcements and a
feeling of 'satisfaction' those acts likely to enhance survival and reproduction..." (33). And finally, human learning
might be rigidly canalized, with individuals only prepared to
learn genetically adaptive cultural messages (34).

One of the principal conclusions of the simplest model
of dual inheritance (30) is that even if the quantitative
capacity for culture is completely shaped by natural selection acting on genes, the observed behavioral traits need not
be those that would be predicted by conventional Neo-
Darwinian reasoning based on the maximization of inclusive
fitness. If this conclusion is correct, then Durham's a
priori argument is incorrect. But to analyze this argument
(35), the model must be extended to represent genetic modifications of cultural fitness by biases or control of the
symmetry of cultural transmission. These effects will be
represented by the expedient of introducing a second specific
culture capacity that has the effect of causing the optimum
of the cultural fitness function to be adjusted by selection
operating on genes.

Results of the Models

A formal model based on these assumptions is given in the appendix. The interested and mathematically adept reader will find the model useful to examine the logical structure of our version of dual inheritance theory. The complexities introduced to evolutionary dynamics by the existence of culture are substantial, and the use of mathematical machinery is the only method by which the complex web of cause and effect inherent in the postulates can be examined rigorously. Even so, the situation is sufficiently complicated that rather artificial models must be employed in order to obtain results. The minimum complexity that has to be introduced is a variable to represent the state of the genetic system, a variable to represent the state of the cultural system, and a variable to represent the relation of the states of the two systems to phenotypes. This contrasts with the usual case in evolutionary biology where much can be learned by considering the properties of evolutionary change at a single genetic locus.

The approach taken in the models in our previous paper and in the appendix is known in population biology as "evolutionary stable strategy" (ESS) analysis (27). The technique involves ignoring the actual time path of evolutionary events and considering only the nature of evolutionary equilibria. The models are analyzed by finding or assuming equilibrium and asking if a given equilibrium strategy is resistant to invasion by a rare genetic or cultural variant. If a new strategy is introduced, will evolution cause it to increase? Such models are easier to analyze than fully dynamic ones, but artifacts are possible. We make these caveats, not so much to apologize for our own results, as to make the point that any facile generalization about the nature of human evolution should be viewed skeptically at this point. The problem is difficult and very much work remains to be done. However, we are convinced that the broad outlines of dual inheritance theory are general and will hold under further analysis.

Even the simple models with only a quantitative capacity for culture predict a variety of results, depending upon conditions. Given the assumptions, they are rather commonsensical. The key criterion for whether or not a given capacity for culture is an ESS is whether or not the equilibrium behavior produced by the joint effects of genes and culture is more fit genetically than genes could achieve in the absence of culture. If the cultural optimum is far from the genetic optimum or if there is a large physiological cost of culture capacity, the presence of a culture capacity is not stable. Thus, a culture capacity will evolve only when culture improves genetic fitness, despite the tendency for culture to respond independently to selection and be energetically costly.

Other conclusions are not quite so obvious. One is that culture may not evolve even if it makes possible phenotypes that are, in the abstract, genetically fitter. Some combinations of genotype and culture cannot evolve because of the existence of two partly competing selective forces. Also, under some circumstances, the ESS phenotype may be at the genetic optimum with partial cultural determination, while in other cases the particular trait may be at the cultural optimum. Traits of this last kind are particularly likely to evolve if the quantitative capacity for culture at equilibrium allows several cultural traits to exist. In this case, the genetic fitness advantage of the culture capacity will be averaged over the effects of many culturally affected traits, and individual elements of culture may be far from the genetic optimum, or even frankly deleterious to genetic fitness. The only requirement is that the average of all cultural traits, at the given capacity for culture, be an ESS.

Incorporating a qualitative capacity for culture that is designed to mimic the effects of genetic controls on the form of cultural fitness by the mechanisms of bias and symmetry has one non-trivial result -- it makes it more rather than less likely that a given trait will be at the cultural rather than the genetic optimum. As the form (as a function of phenotype) of cultural fitness comes to resemble that of genetic fitness more and more closely, culture becomes a more reliable means of genetic optimization. Perhaps more important than this result is the fact that the model illustrates that the coevolutionary optimization logic of the dual inheritance model is preserved when a qualitative rather than a quantitative capacity for culture is introduced. Even under the strongly "sociobiological" assumption that the genetic system optimizes its own fitness by controlling the quantity of cultural inheritance and the details of the form of cultural inheritance, the cultural system will have a measure of independence.

The only way Durham's hypothesis that genes keep culture completely "on track" can be precisely true is if genetic controls, in the form of biases and symmetry, are physiologically costless and sacrifice none of the advantages of culture. In that case, whatever advantages there are to culture will be captured by genes since the capacities for culture will in turn have no genetic fitness costs. However, it is unlikely that such specific capacities are completely costless. Further, it is generally believed that the major advantages of culture include the greater adaptive flexibility of the cultural system. The more culture is hedged with genetic restrictions, the less flexibility there is likely to be. Whether Durham's hypothesis is approximately correct is an empirical question that we will return to in a later section.

These models show that a second system of inheritance poses a substantial evolutionary problem. Its advantages are counter-balanced by a general cost -- selection acting on the second system will have a tendency to cause the phenotype to diverge from the genetic optimum. In certain circumstances, the advantage of the cultural system may outweigh this cost and the capacity for culture will expand. The model results, therefore, suggest why culture is rare, or at least why culture capacities are seldom very large and predicts that in animals with large capacities that genetically nonoptimal traits should be observable. We will give evidence that supports both of these predictions in a following section.

Discussion

The Dynamic Sufficiency of the Model

We argued earlier that none of the commonly held views of the human evolutionary process are logically satisfactory. In Lewontin's (10) more precisely defined terminology, they are not dynamically sufficient. The "all genes" view fails to provide a satisfactorily explicit model of the evolutionary relationship between the manifestly large amount of cultural inheritance in humans and ongoing genetic evolution. The "all culture" view cannot provide a satisfactory account of origins since if culture is utterly independent of genetic fitness, it is hard to see how an organic capacity for culture could arise. The syncretic views of many biologists and social scientists (36) we believe to be correct as far as they go. However, these accounts also fail the dynamic sufficiency criterion because they do not give a mechanistic account of the dynamics of culture and genes and the relationship between the two systems.

Dual inheritance theory overcomes the minimal hurdle of dynamic sufficiency by assuming that the genetic system is controlled by conventional Neo-Darwinian processes, and that the cultural system is controlled by processes analogous to, but rather different in mechanism from, those that operate on the genetic system. The relationship between the two

systems is assumed to be governed by natural selection operating on organic capacities for culture. The models based on
these assumptions are sufficient because they account for and
link together the essential elements determining human phenotype. Although obviously (and necessarily) oversimplified,
the models could conceivably describe the basic features of
the human evolutionary process.

The models are also a useful means to examine the more
extreme positions in the sociobiology debate in light of
empirical evidence. If it can be shown that the benefits of
cultural inheritance are largely preserved when the form of
cultural fitness is tightly controlled by symmetry and bias,
then the predictions of the dual inheritance models approximate those of the "all genes" sociobiologists. On the other
hand, if it can be shown that any control by genes of cultural transmission lowers genetic fitness, then the models
predict the "all culture" conclusion.

Of course, empirical evidence may also show that dual
inheritance theory must be more or less substantially revised or wholly rejected. The reader can quite likely imagine several amendments that will be required to improve
the realism of the models, such as the incorporation of an
explicit theory of learning into the model of cultural
dynamics (37). Nonetheless, we think that the relative
simplicity and generality of the models proposed here are
virtues not to be given up lightly.

Dual Inheritance Theory and
the Nature of Group Differences

The doctrine of the psychic unity of mankind holds that
there are no significant primary (read genetic) differences
in mental function between human races (38). In the balance
of this essay, we will formulate a dual inheritance hypothesis incorporating this doctrine and examine some of the
available evidence which might falsify such an hypothesis.

The first question of interest is whether any version of
the doctrine is plausible in light of the obviously massive
differences in behavior between human groups. Darwin posed
this problem very clearly. In his discussion of races in
Chapter 7 in The Descent of Man, he used the conceit of an
imaginary naive naturalist examining the evidence given by
human races to illustrate one side of the argument. "On
inquiry he would find that they were adapted to live under
widely different climates, and that they differed somewhat
in bodily constitution and mental disposition. If he were

then told that hundreds could be brought from the same
countries, he would assuredly declare that they were as good
species as many to which he had been in the habit of affixing
specific names." Yet after reviewing the evidence pro and
con on the matter, Darwin himself felt forced to conclude
that none of the differences between races of man are of "any
direct or special service to him." To account for such organic differences as do exist, he appealed to the mechanism
of sexual selection, hence the appending of his long general
discussion of this topic to the Descent. The exceptions appeared to Darwin to be the "intellectual and moral faculties." With regard to the evolution of such faculties, he
stressed the effects of "inherited habit," "good education,"
"inculcation by the ablest and best men embodied in the laws,
customs and traditions of the nation" and "public opinion"
all proceeding against a background of "social instincts,"
particularly a susceptibility to the praise and blame of
one's fellows. He traced the evolution of the social instincts under the most primitive tribal conditions he could
imagine and placed their origin at a "very remote period."

In the context of a dual inheritance hypothesis this
question is reformulated in terms of the evolution of
capacities for culture rather than social instincts, but it
is otherwise much the same. Does the modern evidence con-
tradict the ideas that 1) the contemporary capacities are of
long standing and 2) that the selective forces on the capacities have been more or less uniform since their origin?
The alternative hypothesis is that human social behavior and
culture capacities have responded directly to the selective
environments of different times and places. Although most
modern evolutionary biologists have followed Darwin's conclusions about the defensibility of the doctrine of psychic
unity, a few have not. C. D. Darlington (39), for example,
has interpreted the details of even recent human history in
terms of changes in the frequency of genes for leadership,
farming, iron working and so forth. He imagines that behaviors usually interpreted as cultural are the result of
genetic responses to local selective environments. The de-
fenders of a direct genetic explanation for the intergroup
variation of I.Q. are another example of proponents of this
hypothesis in a more limited form. This view is very hard
to support in light of the documented amount of gene flow in
human populations, the general lack of covariation of measurable genetic traits, and the weak correlation of what
variation does exist with cultural groups (40). Moreover,
the documented speed with which radical cultural change has
occurred makes it implausible that genetic evolution could
account for it.

The second question is: Given the doctrine of psychic
unity, how closely and by what mechanisms do capacities for
culture actually control the form of cultural fitness? Can
invariant or only slightly variant genetic capacities ensure
that all important or significant cultural variants optimize
genetic fitness? As outlined earlier in the discussion of
Durham's hypothesis, an affirmative answer to this question
is given by many sociobiologists. However, it is not true,
contrary to the implications of their critics, that most
sociobiologists have seriously challenged psychic unity.
There are two quite distinct forms of an "all genes" hypotheses epitomized by the differences between Durham and
Darlington. For Darlington, the control by genes of behavior
is direct; for sociobiologists it is largely indirect. In
sociobiological terms, genes determine, not behavior itself,
but a behavioral strategy. Consider E. O. Wilson's "genes
for homosexuality" as an example of the difference. In his
longest passage on homosexuality, Wilson (41) equivocates between the hypotheses of direct genetic control of homosexuality and a universal genetic strategy model. The direct
genetic control would involve a polymorphism for homosexual
behavior. The strategy would be a genetic instruction in the
form of: "If you have a small chance of successful reproduction in your particular environment, help your brothers
and sisters raise their children and obtain sexual gratifi-
cation in any manner that minimizes entanglements, including
homosexual unions." There may be little genetic variance
for the strategy, even though only a small fraction of people
actually exhibit homosexual behavior. In a more general context, Wilson (42) clearly emphasizes the overwhelming importance of such invariant strategies producing appropriately
variable outcomes. Similarly, Richard Alexander and Gerald
Borgia (43) have postulated a "supergene" for kin altruism,
which, although it does not vary between populations, can
cause the diversity of observed human kin behavior to be
genetically optimal.

To the extent that such strategies exist, they may also
act to bias cultural inheritance. An individual will sort
among the cultural variants available as models for those
which best implement the genetic strategy (44). From the
perspective of dual inheritance theory, we want to know how
thoroughly and effectively genes manage to control cultural
variation. Recall that the strategy of having cultural
capacities produces a pair of tradeoffs. There is a simple
physiological cost to the anatomical adaptations for culture.
But unique to the dual inheritance situation is the tradeoff
between capturing the benefits of the more flexible system
while tolerating the costs of culture responding independently to its selective environment. Empirically, the

question is whether or not we can discover large benefits to
asymmetric, weakly biased culture capacities and consequently
identify culturally determined behaviors that depart detectably from the genetic optimum.

To investigate these questions, we propose to see if any
evidence contradicts a syncretic dual inheritance hypothesis
that is roughly equidistant between the sociobiological "all
genes" and the "all culture" hypotheses. This hypothesis is
that the advantages of flexibility inherent in the cultural
system are large and universal in Homo sapiens. Thus, the
hypothesis holds that culture capacities are unlikely to differ substantially between groups. On the other hand, we expect that broad, simple genetic controls of culture by the
management of symmetry and the imposition of bias will evolve
to insure that culture, averaged over many traits and many
individuals in many cultures, will be genetically favorable.
Thus cultural behavior will evolve with sufficient independence to be detectably different from expected genetic
optima, but not categorically different, as suggested by the
qualitative results of the dual models. Essentially we imagine that both the costs and benefits of culture are large
in humans and that our phenotypes will be a compromise between the dictates of nature and nurture, even though in the
last analysis, genetic fitness is optimized. In the following sections, we will present several lines of evidence that
are not inconsistent with this hypothesis but that are difficult to reconcile with "all genes" or "all culture"
positions.

Origin of Culture Capacity

From the perspective of modern humans, the adaptive
advantages of culture appear obvious. Enculturation is an
efficient means of storing an adaptive program. By permitting the inheritance of successful learning, it reduces the
cost of trial and error learning. Much more highly sophisticated behaviors can evolve because of the cumulative nature
of cultural evolution than could evolve by simple learning.
Although cultural inheritance is stable enough to accumulate
over successive generations, it is a more flexible and
rapidly responding mechanism of adaptation than simple
genetic determination of phenotype. Dual inheritance theory
suggests that this anthropomorphic attention to the benefits
of a cultural system must be balanced by careful attention to
its disadvantages. In particular, it predicts that the cause
of the origins of a massive capacity for culture must be
sought in special circumstances where particular benefits
outweigh the cost of independent evolution. Only if the
benefits of culture are completely overwhelming (the "all

culture" alternative) or if the costs are controlled at
small sacrifice of the benefits (the "all genes" alternative)
is the evolution of a cultural capacity unproblematic.

The first line of evidence that suggests that the evolution of cultural capacities is indeed problematic comes from
the literature on protoculture in animals. Bennett Galef
(45) provides an excellent review of this literature from
ethology and experimental psychology. The generalizations
he extracts include:

1. The transmission of acquired patterns of behavior
from one individual to another is relatively common in
vertebrates.

2. A great range of complexity exists in animal protoculture, from simple inheritance of territory to the
teaching of novel motor patterns.

3. The adaptive advantages of acquiring the learned
behavior of others can be readily imagined.

4. The kinds of behaviors which can be acquired by
imitation of others are quite restricted in most animals.
Arbitrary tasks are not acquired by imitation of
trained conspecifics.

5. Complex examples of protoculture are rare compared
with simple ones. Cases of communication of novel
motor patterns are particularly rare compared to
acquired modifications of existing patterns.

The dual inheritance model provides a natural explanation of these otherwise somewhat paradoxical facts. Generalizations one and two imply that the preadaptations for cultural inheritance are widespread among vertebrates. Generalization three would seem to indicate that selection should
generally favor an increased importance of cultural transmission in determining phenotype. However, generalizations
four and five indicate the opposite. While common, the
capacity for protocultural transmission is almost always
quite circumscribed.

There would seem to be two conventional evolutionary
explanations for this state of affairs. First, one might
imagine that the physiological costs of increasing the
capacity for cultural inheritance, in terms of increased
brain size for example, might overbalance the benefits that
Galef cites. However, given the wide variety of organisms
involved, with an accompanying great range of behavioral

complexity, it is hard to explain the uniformity with which protocultural inheritance is constrained to narrow ranges of behaviors in almost all species. Second, it might be argued that an expanded cultural capacity depends on an unlikely evolutionary innovation, for example upright posture or generative language, that has only occurred once in the course of evolution and was followed by an episode of posi- tive feedback until modern humans resulted. While this argument is certainly plausible, it is a kind of evolu- tionist's deus ex machina that can be used to explain any otherwise inexplicable adaptation. It should be accepted only if directly adaptive explanations can be ruled out.

In contrast, generalizations one through five are a natural result of the syncretic dual inheritance hypothesis. The most general prediction of the model is that even if a more elaborate capacity for cultural inheritance makes pos- sible more fit organisms, as Galef argues, an increase of capacity for culture will not necessarily be selected for. The additional condition, that the behavioral equilibrium resulting from the interaction of the genetic and cultural evolutionary process must be genetically optimal, must also obtain. Since the dynamic of natural selection acting on culture will in general cause this equilibrium to be dif- ferent from what selection on genes alone would create, the nature of the dual inheritance process imposes an additional evolutionary cost on the evolution of the capacity for culture. Roughly put, the genetic cost of the cultural evolutionary process is the inescapable tendency of the culturally determined component of phenotype to go its own way. We believe this cost is inescapable because it results from the same features of a cultural inheritance system that produce its benefits -- a difference in the mechanism by which the determinants of adaptation are transmitted from individual to individual.

A corollary of this argument is that we would be more likely to observe cultural inheritance in cases where the process is restricted to traits for which the genetic and cultural fitnesses will be quite similar. Thus it is widely reported that food and habitat choice are inherited cultural- ly, often in a quite restricted fashion (46). The cultural inheritance of novel motor patterns and arbitrary social or sexual behavior, for which non-parental inheritance could cause cultural and genetic fitness to diverge substantially, seem to be excluded in all organisms except man.

Interpreting these generalizations about protocultural behavior in terms of the two capacities model presented here provides an interesting empirical problem for the "all genes"

hypothesis, at least as it can be formulated in terms of the
dual inheritance model. Recall that the two capacities model
provides a genetically controlled trait, the qualitative
capacity that modifies cultural fitness. Thus genetic
selection acting on this capacity can cause the outcome of
cultural selection to be the same as genetic. The key tradeoff, determining the genetically optimal value of the
qualitative capacity, is the extent to which the benefits of
cultural inheritance, for example its flexibility, are lost
by constraining the cultural inheritance process. The
generalizations above, when taken in context of the dual
inheritance model, imply that for most organisms the costs of
qualitative controls for more complex traits (arbitrary motor
skills, social and sexual behavior) usually exceed the benefits, and the capacities do not evolve at all. Thus in order
to maintain the "all genes" hypothesis for humans, one must
suppose that unlike protocultural organisms, the human
genetic system has some unique means of controlling the
cultural-selective process for complex traits without
sacrificing the benefits. To maintain the "all culture"
hypothesis on the other hand, one supposes that there is some
extraordinary benefit to humans that compensates for the fact
that the cultural selective criteria will be in general quite
different for complex traits.

As an aside, the dual inheritance logic should be generally applicable to the evolution of any organism whose
phenotype is simultaneously determined by two different
systems of inheritance -- different in the sense that they
have different life cycles. Such double systems are
ubiquitous in nature, although seldom important. The genetic
systems of ordinary organisms have two major examples of dual
inheritance, extra-chromosomal loci and the sex chromosomes.
As in the case of culture, if genetic material on the Y sex
chromosome could code for a modification in the sex ratio,
then there would be a very strong selection on that system
of inheritance to increase the fraction of the heterogametic
sex, even though the optimal sex ratio for the autosomal
genome was one half. Maynard-Smith (47) cites the existence
of just such a case. Similarly, the rules of inheritance
for extrachromosomal loci differ from those for chromosomal
loci, and the optimal phenotype for transmitting such loci
is, in general, not the same as for the autosomal genome
since traits coded on mitochondria and chloroplasts are inherited maternally (48). The extra-nuclear system could thus
increase its fitness by increasing the fraction of females.
Not surprisingly, only a very small fraction of the total
genome is transmitted by either of these structures. These
systems provide additional confirmation of the model pre-

diction that the existence of two code systems of roughly
coordinate importance requires rather special conditions.

The second line of evidence is that of human paleon-
tology and paleoarcheology which suggests that the origin of
large capacities for culture is an adaptation to the fluctuating, unstable climate of the Pleistocene. The environment of the Pleistocene is the kind of circumstance that is
likely to provide a large selective advantage for culture in
spite of its cost. If the conventional view of climate
history is correct (49), the variance of climatic fluctuations on time scales of the order of tens and hundreds of
thousands of years increased dramatically beginning perhaps
two million years ago. The speed and flexibility of cultural
inheritance is presumably able to track these fluctuations
much more effectively than could the genetic system.

Models of human origins frequently view the process as
one of positive feedback between anatomical modification and
the evolving capacity for culture (50) triggered by the
evolution of upright posture and the freeing of hands for
tool use. For this hypothesis the evolution of culture
capacity is, in itself, unproblematic. Its development is
a product of an accidental preadaptive breakthrough. We
critized hypotheses like this on epistemological grounds
above. The empirical problem with it is that bipedal
Australopithecines apparently existed perhaps two million
years before major increases in brain size and extensive use
of tools is evident in the record (51). The Oldowan tool
culture and the first evidence of Homo grade hominids seem
to coincide with the climatic deterioration of the early
Pleistocene, rather than with the earlier evolution of the
bipedal preadaptation. In addition, the continued development of hominids and their culture in the middle Pleistocene
(52) was associated with an increase in the intensity of
climatic fluctuations beginning about a million years ago
(53). On this interpretation of the cause for the origin
and development of Homo grade culture capacity, preadaptation
was a subordinate effect. The accidents of history may have
determined which organism responded most quickly and successfully to the increasingly variable environment, but in the absence of an environment selecting for the advantages of culture, the preadaptations would have remained preadaptations.

If the primary advantage of cultural inheritance is the
rapid tracking of fluctuating environments, it is unlikely
that major differences in culture capacities would arise
between groups. It is now reasonably clear that the
Pleistocene climatic fluctuations profoundly affected the
whole globe. In particular, the evidence is that tropical

environments were quite unstable (54). They were not calm
refuges where evolution could proceed unaffected by the
subarctic and temperate glaciers. Insofar as the genetic
advantage of a capacity for culture is flexibility, the
world-wide nature of these events means that selection for
culture-capacity is likely to have been similar everywhere
and adaptations to local environments encoded largely by
the cultural system.

The Nature of Culture Capacity

This evidence on the origin of culture capacity is certainly consistent with the doctrine of psychic unity and the
specific syncretic model we have outlined. But given the
necessarily sketchy nature of the direct evidence on the
origin-of-culture events, other interpretations are clearly
possible. Our hypothesis would also tend to be supported by
evidence that the structure of genetic capacities for culture
is fairly strong but simple and rather nonspecific. By contrast, if bias and symmetry controls of cultural acquisition
are very weak, some form of "all culture" hypothesis is indicated, but if quite detailed, some form of "all genes" hypothesis. This issue has been examined in many contexts in
the social sciences and biology, including the issue of genes
and I.Q. discussed previously. Perhaps the most interesting
for understanding the genetic control of behavior and culture capacity is the pattern of human cognitive development.

Empirically, humans exhibit a developmental sequence of
cognitive capacities with age. Structural theories which
account for the stages as an invariant unfolding of capacities with age, implying a large role for genes, have been
advanced (55). If such stages exist, and if the structures
produced account for most of human behavior, the sociobiological "all genes" hypothesis is perhaps correct. Two
separate problems face typical structural theories. First,
since the structures are usually pictured as human universals, they provide no account of between-group variability.
Either the structuralists must allow for genetic variation
between groups or they must attribute the differences to
different learning environments -- the universal strategy
model. Second, there is the evidence reviewed by Rosenthal
and Zimmerman (56) that social learning plays the major role
in cognitive development. They cite many examples of ex-
periments which cast doubt on the existence of innate determination of cognitive development by showing that the normal
sequence can be advanced or reversed by social learning.
They interpret these findings as indicating that mental development is largely a matter of the accumulation of culturally acquired skills by largely unstructured young minds.

Robert LeVine's (57) conclusions from psychological anthropology were similar and led to his acceptance of Campbell's
explicitly Darwinian view of culture. Because of the empirical difficulties of disentangling genetic and cultural effects on human behavior, this issue will not soon be solved
exactly, but the existing state of the evidence does not
favor any "all genes" hypothesis.

On the other hand, some genetically determined controls
of culture acquisition do exist. The simplest is the very
long juvenile period of humans. We grow very slowly and remain physically dependent on and subordinate to adults for
an extraordinarily long period. One consequence of this
form of life history is that a large proportion of our basic
cultural skills and values are usually acquired in our natal
household, typically a disproportionate share from our biological parents. This in turn assures that cultural inheritance is reasonably symmetric, producing the empirical
problem of parcelling out inherited variance into genetic and
cultural components, as well as ensuring that the selective
optima of genes and culture are not too different. The long
human juvenile period entails two costs. The energetic costs
of raising slow growing offspring are considerable, as any
animal breeder can attest. And the tendency to restrict
cultural acquisition of basic attitudes and skills to a small
set of close relatives reduces the flexibility of the cultural system substantially, particularly if the cultural behavior acquired at early ages is relatively resistant to
modification in adulthood. Since some pathologies like
alcoholism and child abuse are apparently stable cultural
acquisitions acquired in childhood, this cost seems
real.

Whatever the reality of more complex genetic structures
turns out to be, it is clear that the degree of symmetry
imposed on cultural inheritance is sufficient to rule out an
"all culture" hypothesis of the form proposed by Sahlins.
In fact, neither an "all culture" or "all genes" position of
the structuralist sort can easily account for the long dependence of human juveniles. If biases based on innate
structures can control the acquisition of culture accurately
or if genetic strategies plus reason and learning are the
dominant effect, it is difficult to see why the energetic
cost of a long juvenile period need to borne. An "all genes"
hypothesis thus seems to require a very strong dependence on
symmetry controls to account for the human life cycle. If
the flexibility of culture is so overwhelmingly important
that genetic controls are minimized, it is difficult to account for a pattern of enculturation that ensures a quite
detectable covariance of the two systems. Only some form

of intermediate hypothesis is consistent with such strong
but very general control of culture.

The evidence from protocultural animals supports the
human evidence on this point. Advanced protocultural animals like the ground-living monkeys and chimpanzees have long
juvenile periods, and the ability of many other protocultural
animals to acquire behavior is restricted to juveniles. For
example, the acquisition of song repertoire in sparrows occurs within 10 days of hatching, even though the young sparrows do not sing until a month later (58). In both rats and
in Japanese macaques acquisition of food preferences are restricted to juveniles (59). Under normal circumstances,
young macaques acquire food preferences from parents but if
some novel food substance is introduced, the young can independently acquire a taste for the novel food, which is then
passed on to their offspring and thus spreads through the
group (60). This process is more flexible than either strict
de novo learning by each individual, or genetically coded
food preferences. However, the restriction of social learning to an early age allows a less flexible phenotype than a
generalized ability to acquire food preferences at any age.
Clearly when a novel food is introduced, adults could benefit by utilizing it, and if they could acquire a preference
for the novel food either by de novo learning or by imitation, it would be beneficial. Again, these results suggest
that an asymmetric culture capacity is genetically costly and
likely to be restricted. But they also suggest that the
benefits of culture are largely its increased flexibility, so
that controls on the form of cultural fitness tend to be
broad and general rather than detailed specifications for
those traits for which cultural inheritance is any advantage
at all. Our own intuition is that in humans the genetic controls of culture capacity are restricted to the few mechanisms that can be simultaneously simple, general, and highly
effective. Besides the long dependent juvenile period ensuring a reasonably symmetrical system, there are probably
genetic predilections that act as bias mechanisms, including
such things as pleasurable sex and infant bonding. Only such
a system of genetic controls could maintain a tolerable approximation of genetically adaptive behavior in the cultural system while capturing very much of its flexibility advantages.

The Cultural Basis of Intergroup Variation

So far we have spoken rather generally of the advantages
a cultural system of inheritance confers on an organism via a
flexible and speedy response to changing environments. The
specific issue of interest is still the spectacular behavioral polymorphism of the human species. The question is how

the cultural mechanism, particularly if it is rather weakly
constrained by genes, can produce what seemed to Darwin's
naive naturalist to be good species. We will first consider
the potential mechanisms for the efficient evolution of local
specializations and then consider the specific case of human
kinship behavior.

The first thing to note is that a substantial fraction
of human behavioral diversity is adaptive. Among simpler
human societies, subsistence strategies and their correlates
in social organization are clearly systematic cultural
adaptations to local environmental circumstances. A large
body of literature in ecological anthropology has developed
documenting these adaptations (61).

Local specialization based on a genetic system appears
to require the erection of barriers to gene flow to be effective, particularly when the specialists are sympatric or
nearly so. For this reason, evolutionary biologists have
long been concerned with the processes by which speciation
takes place (62). Departing from an existing fitness optimum by range extension (63) or speciation is apparently a
severe evolutionary problem. The conventional picture of
evolution of major novelty by allopatric speciation depends
upon geographical isolating barriers and hence, perhaps, on
geological accidents for its efficacy. Thus genetic inheritance systems are rather conservative in their ability
to respond to changing conditions with wholly new adaptive
types (species) compared to the ability to respond to minor
environmental changes. Even insects, which speciate with
relative abandon, appear to require special circumstances to
radiate (64).

One major adaptive advantage the cultural system may
have evolved to favor is an efficient alternative to the
clumsy genetic process of speciation. Individuals inheriting
their behavior culturally should belong to a conservative
culture pool analogous to the gene pool. If there are
factors which cause such "culture pools" to be more easily
isolated from one another than gene pools, then the capacity
for culture would make possible many specialized cultural
"pseudo-species" without genetic isolation. Language and
other symbolic behaviors like religious ritual are obvious
candidates for isolating factors. Symbol systems are
ideally suited to the rapid differentiation of groups since
they change easily by random drift (symbols are arbitrary)
yet remain useful within a group because of extreme frequency dependent selective retention (symbols must be conventional). Groups of humans transmitting culture by a
complex language will evolve mutually unintelligible dialects

very rapidly compared to a rate at which evolutionary drift
and differential selection would permit the evolution of in-
compatible genotypes. Other mechanisms are possible. We
have explored a nonlinear cultural inheritance system that
gives rise to a resistance to the effect of immigrant individuals (28). Cultural barriers also may be effective at
maintaining basic cultural differences while permitting the
diffusion of selected cultural traits across the barrier (65).
This mechanism is the cultural analog of genetic intro-
gression, a form of evolutionary flexibility present in
plants but normally absent in animals.

If one assumes that genetic controls provide only general
constraints on human cultural inheritance -- desire for
physical comfort, love of children, and loyalty towards kin --
then one can imagine that selection acting on culturally isolated groups would produce culturally determined behavior
that departs significantly from what would be predicted by
inclusive fitness maximization but which nonetheless would be
favored because gene flow also prevented the genetic optimum
from being realized by means of genetic specialization. Thus
it is plausible that the radiation of cultures in the late
Pleistocene and early Recent periods resulted from such a
cultural "speciation" process which favored geographic
specialization in food foraging people. Early and middle
Paleolithic peoples appear, judging from their tool as-
semblages, to have been culturally similar, geographically
wide-spread but rather restricted in their local specializations. It is intriguing that such hominids probably had a
much less elaborate capacity for language than modern humans
(66). Late Paleolithic cultures, by contrast, became highly
specialized and spread to every habitable corner of the
earth (52).

As an aside, this discussion suggests another interesting
evolutionary question: If it is not for the purpose of cultural "pseudo-speciation," how does one explain the human
capacity for learning a great diversity of languages? It has
been noted that whatever deep structure (presumably genetically coded) that exists, provides only very general constraints on the grammar and vocabulary of human language (62).
One would presume that a more restrictive "shallow" structure
would have numerous advantages. It would make language easier to learn and to use. Given some flexibility to adjust
vocabulary for local ecological and social conditions, any
one language would seem to suffice, yet we have thousands.

We now want to return to one of the most important predictions of the syncretic dual inheritance hypothesis. If
the hypothesis is correct, culturally determined behavior

should exhibit systematic deviations from that which would
be predicted from genetic fitness considerations alone. The
hypothesis predicts that, in order to capture the benefits of
flexibility, the selection for culture capacity will permit
substantial asymmetry in the cultural system, and the result
of this asymmetry will be behavior that departs from the
genetic optimum for some traits.

Human behavior towards kin provides a useful set of data
to test this prediction. The evolutionary biologists' theory
of kin selection (68) gives reasonably strong predictions
regarding the nature of the genetically optimal behavior.
Because kinship was found to be so important in human social
organization and so variable between human groups, anthropologists have made it one of the centerpieces of ethnology
and of theoretical discussions. Kin behavior has also been
one of the chief empirical foci in the debate over the
application of sociobiological theory to humans. As Marshall
Sahlins (69) aptly observed "whether the scientific sociobiology will succeed in its ambition of incorporating the
human sciences depends largely on the fate of its theory of
kin selection." Sahlins believes that the evidence from
human kinship shows that it must fail. On the other hand,
the human preoccupation with relatedness gives sociobiologists some comfort (70). The issue turns on the interpretation of details of the data.

Three broad generalizations can be extracted from the
anthropological literature on the subject (71):

a. In most societies, kin altruism forms the basis for
cooperative social and economic behavior.

b. Human kinship behavior is more often than not biased
toward cooperation with relatives genetically descended
from one parent but not the other. Kinship, as reckoned
by a majority of the world's peoples, does not corres-
pond very accurately to genealogy. Cooperation and
altruism are often directed to distantly related
individuals within a descent group and withheld from
closely related ones outside the descent group.

c. The extent and direction, i.e. toward the matriline
or patriline is extremely variable between human groups.
Moreover, behavior can change very rapidly.

On the face of the matter, these data suggest that a compromise between "all genes" and "all culture" interpretations
will be required. Generalization a supports the idea that
genetic kin selection plays some role in human behavior. On

the other hand, generalization c clearly implies that culture
is important. The crux of the issue is the explanation of
b. Sahlins explains b as resulting from "cultural reason,"
although he is not at all specific about just why humans vary
their kinship behavior the way they do (in fact, Sahlins wants
to deny that any mechanistic explanation is satisfactory).
Sociobiologists have given a series of special explanations
for the most important variants of human kin behavior (72).
Their general idea is that these "distorted" patterns are
mechanisms for implementing genetic kin altruism when the
benefits and costs of altruism are affected by local ecological circumstances. These models all assume something
like Alexander and Borgia's (43) kin altruism "supergene"
that ensures optimal behavior in local circumstances.

A general problem with these explanations is that there
is a certain ad hoc quality to them. Since it is well known
that some sort of adaptive or functional explanation can be
developed to account for any behavioral or anatomical
peculiarity, it is important to entertain alternative hypotheses and search for critical data to support or reject
each (73).

The dual inheritance explanation for generalization b
is such an alternative. It is a straightforward extension
of the logic of kin altruism to the cultural system of
inheritance. First, we assume that kinship behavior is an
example of a culturally inherited trait that is constrained
to be acquired at an early age. Further, suppose that in
various societies there is a sexual bias in the cultural
transmission, i.e. offspring are more likely to learn kinship behavior from one parent (or his/her relatives) than
from the other parent. This will lead to a sexually asymmetric pattern of cultural relatedness by common descent,
analogous to the effect of haploid-diploid sex determination
in hymenoptera. Thus kin selection acting on culturally
inherited traits will select for sexually biased and in the
extreme, unilineally organized behavior if there is a
sexual asymmetry in cultural inheritance. Human kin behavior
may thus depart from the predictions derived from considerations of the genetic optimum, this "distortion" being caused
by the cultural optimum being distinctly different from the
genetic.

A matrilineal system will serve as an example. Assume
that there is some local ecological advantage to female
cooperation, say for purposes of agricultural labor. This
situation may tend to lead to new families settling pre-
ferentially with the wife's kin group to preserve established
patterns of cooperation. The result will be that children

will be disproportionally enculturated by the mother's relatives rather than the father's. Hence, culturally, children will be more closely related to mother's kin than to
father's, and "distorted" patterns of altruism will be
selectively favored. The patrilineal case simply assumes
the opposite initial ecological advantage for cooperation
between the sexes.

We have performed simple calculations (74) that show
that this model is at least internally consistent. Which
hypothesis do the available data best support? While a
complete review is not possible in the space of this paper,
the following examples give an indication of the problems
with the sociobiological "all genes" hypothesis. These
hypotheses rely strongly on the question of paternity uncertainty. While it is not simple to determine who fathers
a child, there is seldom any doubt who the mother is. This
fact leads to the differences in reproductive strategies of
the two sexes (75) in ordinary organisms. In most mammals
and many birds, males play little or no role in raising
offspring. Richard Alexander, Penelope Greene and Jeffrey
Kurland (76) have argued that matrilineal systems result
when human male's confidence in his paternity falls so low
that he is more closely related to his sister's children
than he is to his own. Mildred Dickeman (77), on the other
hand, has argued that the extremes of female seclusion, concern for virginity and the like that often accompany
strongly patrilineal systems are a tactic to ensure that
paternity is correctly assessed so that male contribution to
child rearing can be high.

At least some data are available from studies of the
inheritance of blood types that address this question. In
mass surveys of the blood type of putative parents and offspring in studies in the U.S., errors of paternity appear to
be well under ten percent (78). Since American culture is
entirely free of extremes of female seclusion, has high
divorce rates, and is predominately concentrated in urban
areas where philandering is difficult to detect, these data
are surprisingly low. To justify the costly extremes of
Middle Eastern purdah and Chinese foot-binding customs on the
basis of increasing paternity certainty above the 95 to 98%
range achievable in the modern urban West seems a bit extreme. The Yanomamo Indians who have a distinctly patrilineal descent rule, but rather weak marriage bonds and
fairly high rates of promiscuity, have a rate of paternity
error of about 9% (79). On the other hand, Greene's and
Alexander's calculations (72) show that paternity error
must rise to the vicinity of 70% before men are more nearly
related to their sister's than their own putative offspring.

Although the requisite data do not seem to be available for matrilineal societies, one's suspicion might be that the rates of uncertainty ought not to be drastically higher in a relatively tolerant, anonymous urban societies like our own than in a small, intimate, traditional village where efficient gossip networks make it possible for everyone to have a reasonable knowledge of each other's sexual activity.

On the other hand, George Murdock's (80) discovery of a strong statistical association between postmarital residence, descent ideology and kinship terminology support the dual inheritance hypothesis. Cultural relatedness and the patterns of cooperation based on it should be closely related to the makeup of the effective enculturating unit. Patrilineal descent is strongly associated with patrilocal residence, matrilineal descent with matrilocal residence and bilateral descent with neolocal residence. The extremes of female seclusion and male-female role differentiation in some patrilineal societies are more plausibly attributed to selection for high cultural relatedness among the males (lineage solidarity) by reduction of boy's exposure to mother's male relatives (seclusion) and reduction of boys chances of using females as cultural models (a strong ideology of sex role differentiation) than to the apparently small decrease in paternity uncertainty than can be achieved if "normal" paternity uncertainty ranges below 10%. Similarly, weak marriage bonds and relatively high rates of sexual promiscuity are likely to result from, rather than cause, "distorted" patterns of kin altruism in matrilineal societies. The small range in paternity uncertainty that apparently exists is better explained as a result rather than a cause of cultural differences.

Conclusion

Some form of dual inheritance theory is the only logically complete account of the evolutionary behavior of a culture-bearing organism. Even quite simple mathematical models based on the theory give predictions in broad agreement with the behavior of human beings and protocultural organisms and what is known about their origins. Competing hypotheses are limiting cases of dual inheritance theory that, we have argued, require unrealistic assumptions about the form or parameter values of the models or produce empirically false predictions from them. If dual inheritance models are a correct first approximation of the evolutionary dynamics of the human species, they illustrate how the great variety of human "minds" might arise within a single species whose organic variation is strictly limited. Natural selection, or perhaps other processes, operating on cultural

rather than genetic variation can produce adaptations. The
critical prediction of dual inheritance theory is that the
cultural mode of adaptations is inherently costly and that
these costs will take the concrete form of widespread cultural behaviors that are detectably and systematically different from predictions based on considerations of genetic
fitness alone.

The specific hypothesis we have examined is a dual inheritance version of a position orginally developed by
Darwin and eloquently defended by Dobzhansky, among other
modern biologists. We think that underpinning this position
with an explicit mechanism strengthens its central conclusion: The variation between the behavior of human groups almost certainly arises from cultural rather than genetic processes and, although genes may ensure that human behavior
remains generally adaptive, it is also unlikely that genes
directly control the details of our behavior.

Acknowledgments

We are indebted to William Davis, Tom Dietz, Tom Love,
David Wilson, Ted Cloak and William Durham for their useful
criticism of early drafts of this paper. A. L. Caplan's
detailed critique of the penultimate draft was quite useful.
Our discussions with Ronald Pulliam and Donald Campbell of
the issues raised in this paper were most enlightening.
Joan Silk gave the paper a much needed final proofreading.
Delores DuMont's devotion to the typing of the all-too-
numerous drafts of this paper was indispensable. We also
thank L. L. Cavalli-Sforza and M. W. Feldman for allowing us
to attend their class on cultural evolution at Stanford University, Winter 1978.

Appendix

The "Two-Trait" Model

Consider a hypothetical organism with two metric traits: one physiological trait, labeled P, coded by genes and one behavioral trait, labeled B, coded by both genes and culture. Assume that the genetic (W_g) and cultural (W_c) fitnesses of the organism are completely determined by the values of these two traits. These functions are assumed to be quasi-concave. We further assume that the evolutionary possibilities of the organisms are constrained by a set of possible phenotypes, defined by the expression:

$$h(P, B, n) \leq 0 \qquad (1)$$

where $n(0 \leq n \leq 1)$ is a variable that represents the capacity for culture. h is assumed to be concave and not to contain the values P and B that globally maximize either W_c or W_g.

Finally assume that W_g is of such a form that if cultural selection causes B to depart from the genetic optimum, that the maximum of W_g still lies on the boundary of the set of possible phenotypes.

These assumptions taken together formalize several important concepts:

(1) The assumption of a constraint on the possible phenotypes formalizes the common sense notion that there are evolutionary tradeoffs. Forelimbs that are well suited to locomotion will not be suited for tool manipulation or expressing a complex gestural repertoire (81).

(2) The concavity of h and quasi-concavity of W_g and W_c imply that there are diminishing marginal returns to progressive improvements -- as the organism evolves towards limbs more specialized for locomotion, it gains less with each increment -- which in turn guarantees that there is a unique optimum value of P and B for culture and genes. Clearly such unimodal fitness does not characterize every situation; however, assuming it will simplify the discussion with little loss in generality.

(3) The assumption that the solution always lies on the boundary will allow us to find P as a function of

B and thus reduce the problem to one dimension, that of finding the equilibrium value of B and n. Given B, the value of P is determined by the relation $h(P, B, n) = 0$. This facilitates a graphical solution to the model.

(4) The capacity for culture affects the fitness of the organism by modifying h, the set of possible phenotypes -- for example by making new behaviors possible and reducing the physiological possibilities.

If W_g and W_c are sufficiently close, and we argue in the main text that there are evolutionary forces making them so, the situation is shown in Figure 1(a). The hypothetical effect of h on the set of possible phenotypes is shown in Figure 1(b).

To complete the model we must specify how genes and culture interact to determine B. To do this, let g represent the genetic message and c the cultural message. The B is assumed to be given by:

$$B = n \, c + (1 - n)g \qquad (2)$$

Clearly the behaviors specified by (2) must be possible, that is they lie on $H(B, P, n) = 0$. Given $h(B^o, 0, n) = 0$, we can solve for $B^o = B^o (n)$ which gives the intersection of the line defined by $h(B, P, n) = 0$ with $P = 0$ axis as a function of n. We require that B^o have form:

$$B^o = n \, B_2 = (1 - n)B_1 \qquad (3)$$

and

$$0 \leq c \leq B_2; \; 0 \leq g \leq B_1$$

In our previous paper (30), we allowed a considerably more general relation between g, c, n and phenotypes. This approach would be similarly possible here. However, while there would be some gains in generality, such a discussion would be necessarily much more involved.

We assume that c is under the influence of cultural selection and g and n are under the influence of genetic natural selection. Assuming unimodal fitness functions, the only evolutionarily stable phenotype (ESS) can be found by solving the simultaneous maximization problem.

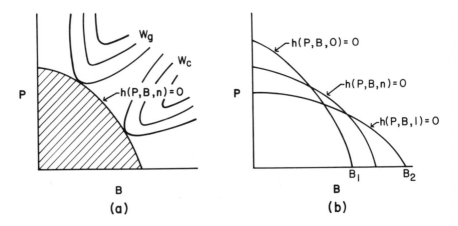

Figure 1.   (a)   The shaded area shows the set of possible
phenotypes for an intermediate value of n and contours
of constant genetic (W_g) and cultural (W_c) fitness.
(b)   Shows how the boundary of the set of possible
phenotypes might vary with n.

$$\max_{n, g} W_g(P, B, n) \qquad (4)$$

$$\max_{c} W_c(P, B, n) \qquad (5)$$

subject to the constraints given by relation (1) - (3).

The assumption that n is under the control of natural selection on genotype was made because it seemed appropriate to the problem of the evolution of cultural behavior in animals or man. This is not a fundamental precept, only a preliminary assertion.

The model described in this section is in some respects formally similar to the usual microeconomic model of a firm producing two joint products. B and P would represent the quantities produced of the two products, $h(., ., .)$ the production possibilities frontier and W_g and W_c two competing but related corporate goals, say profit and market share. The dual inheritance model differs, of course, in the ways that these goals are resolved. The frequent analogy between microeconomic and evolutionary models has been reviewed by Hirschleifer (82).

We will rely on graphical analysis to solve the problem posed by expressions (1) - (5). First n is assumed to be fixed and the evolutionary equilibrium that results from selection acting on the genetic and cultural codes is found. Thus for each value of n there is a value of genetic fitness, W_g associated with the ESS. Finally, we determine the value of n that maximizes W_g.

Equation (2) and the unimodality of W_g, W_c in B insure that $W_g(g, c)$ and $W_c(g, c)$ are straight, parallel "ridges" as shown in Figure 2(a). Since the assumption that natural selection acting on genes causes g to change in the direction of increasing W_g and similarly for c and W_c, in this example the ESS is that shown in Figure 2(b).

For each value of n there is a value of B that maximizes W_g; call it B_g. Similarly B_c maximizes W_c. For expositional convenience, we will assume throughout that $B_c > B_g$. The reverse case creates no difficulties (30). With this assumption

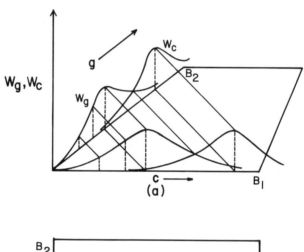

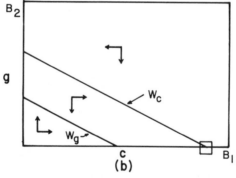

Figure 2.   (a)   Shows a perspective view of genetic fitness,
   W_g, and cultural fitness, W_c, as functions of genotype,
   g, and culture-type c.   The lines drawn on the two
   ridges and parallel to them are lines of equal phenotype as a function of g and c.   (b)   The straight lines,
   labeled W_g and W_c, are, respectively, the combinations
   of g and c that maximize W_g and W_c, as they are shown in
   2(a).   The arrows represent the signs of the rates of g
   and c under the action of cultural and genetic selection.   To arrive at the form shown return to 2(a) and
   assume c climbs up hill on W_c and g climbs W_g.

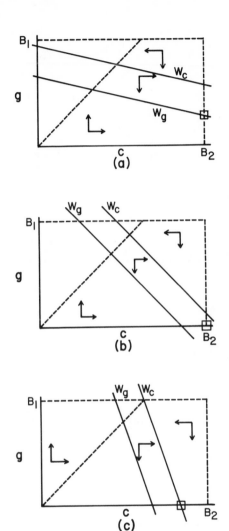

Figure 3. Shows three different evolutionary stable phenotypes for different increasing values of n.
(a) B_g (b) $B_C > B > B_g$ (c) B_C; where B_g and B_C are
respectively the values of B that maximize W_g and W_C at
a given value of n. A fourth possible case $B_g > B_1$ has
been neglected. In each case W_g goes through the point
(B_g, B_g) and W_C through (B_C, B_C). Note however that
B_g and B_C are not necessarily constant for (a) through
(c).

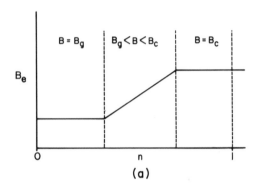

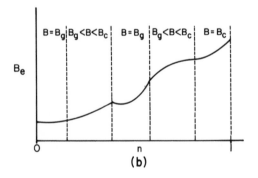

Figure 4. (a) Shows the variation of evolutionary stable phenotype with n for the one-trait model described in (3). (b) Shows one example path for $B_e(n)$ for the two-trait model described here. Because B_c and B_g now vary, there are a variety of possible paths.

there are three classes of evolutionarily stable pheontypes, labeled B_e, shown in Figure 3.

Our previous model showed that for the one trait model the lines W_g, W_c rotated around fixed points, the optimum phenotypes, as n was increased from zero to one. As a result the evolutionarily stable phenotype, B_e, as a function of n, must have the form shown in Figure 4(a). For the two trait model described here, things are no longer quite so simple. The lines still rotate (the slope of the lines is -n) however, since the optimal phenotype B_c and B_g vary, the lines do not rotate about a fixed point. Thus B_e as a function of n is made of segments of the three different classes of solutions $B_e = B_g$, $B_g < B_e < B_c$, $B_e = B_c$ and could have a complex form such as that shown in Figure 4(b). However, we will assume for "reasonable" specifications of h(B, P, n), W_g and W_c, the ESS will begin at B_g and then shift to B_c much as shown in Figure 4(a).

Figure 5 shows how we will use this information to graphically determine the evolutionarily stable phenotype. Part (a) shows the underlying assumption that increasing culture capacity is costless -- that is, increasing cultural control of behavior makes possible both more adaptive physiologies and more adaptive behavior. One might suppose that cultural inheritance makes more flexible and adaptive behaviors possible and at the same time allows the organism to dispense with the neurophysiology necessary to code for complicated instinctual behavior. Given that cultural inheritance is such an unmixed blessing, one might guess that evolution would favor complete cultural control over behavior, i.e., n=1. <u>A central message of this model is that this is not the case</u>.

Figures 5(b) and 5(c) show contour maps of $W_g(B, n)$ and $W_c(B, n)$. The solid lines represent the genetically and culturally optimal phenotypes as functions of n, i.e., $B_g(n)$ and $B_c(n)$. Figure 5(d) again plots $W_g(B, n)$ but superimposed on it is the line $B_c(n)$ taken from 5(c). Recall we assume that typically $B_e(n)$ follows $B_g(n)$ for a distance, then transfers to $B_c(n)$. This path is shown by the arrows in Figure 5(c).

W_g is maximized at the point marked B_e*. Thus a value

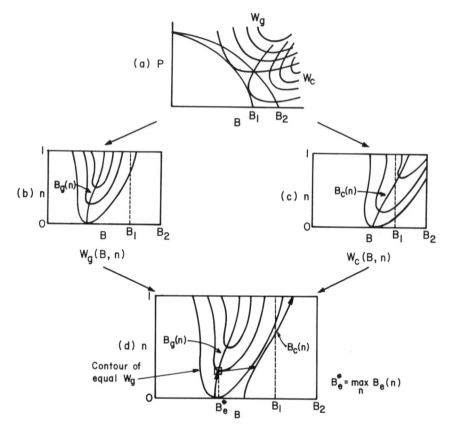

Figure 5.   This figure illustrates the graphical method for
determining the evolutionary stable phenotype.   (a) The
form of the set of possible phenotypes h(P, B, n) shown
represents the case in which the capacity for culture is
physiologically costless.   (b) Since the genetically
optimal phenotypes lie on the boundary of h, we can find
W_g as a function of B and n.   A contour map of W_g (B, n)
is drawn in 5(b).   The line labeled B_g(n) is the genetically optimal phenotype as a function of n.   5(c) similarly shows contours of constant W_c as a function of B
and n.   The line labeled B_c(n) is the culturally optimal
phenotype as a function of n.   (d) Again W_g(B, n) is
plotted as in (b) but superimposed on it is B_c(n) from
(c).   We have assumed that the evolutionary stable
phenotype as a function of n is of the form shown in
Figure 4(a).   To find B_e(n) follow the arrows.   The ESS
is generated by finding the maximum of W_g along the path
B_e(n).   It is shown as the boxed point.

of n less than one is evolutionarily stable <u>even though</u> <u>increasing n uniformly makes more fit organisms an abstract</u> <u>possibility</u>. The reason for this curious behavior is also evident. As culture capacity is increased, a point is reached where genetic specification can no longer balance cultural specification so that the result is the genetic optimum. Beyond this point the cultural code "captures" the phenotype and selection (on culture) acts to maximize cultural fitness. <u>The genetically more fit phenotypes are</u> <u>possibilities that cannot be achieved by simultaneous selec-</u> <u>tion on genes and culture because of the coevolutionary</u> <u>dynamic of the dual inheritance process.</u>

Given the many possible forms of h, W_g and W_c plus the possibility of complicated switching back and forth between B_g and B_c, the model can generate a wide range of behaviors. Following are some interesting examples and observations about the causes of the various behaviors:

1. If there is a significant physiological cost as-sociated with increasing the capacity for culture, the model will result in n near 0. This result is shown in Figure 6(a). The increase in possible behavior does not compensate for the decrease in physiology. Clearly a continuum of cases is possible from that shown in 6(a) to that in Figure 5, including cases in between where genetic fitness is more or less neutral to changes in n.

2. The greater the differences between the genetically and culturally optimal phenotypes relative to the "steepness" of W_g, the less likely it is that the ESS will be the culturally optimal phenotype. This is shown in Figure 6(b). Intuitively, the culturally optimal phenotype will be observed when the cost due to cultural selection going its way is small compared to the benefit due to a generally improved phenotype.

3. As shown in Figure 7(a), evolutionarily stable phenotypes intermediate between the genetic and cultural optimum are possible.

4. Figure 7(b) shows that multiple ESS's are possible. The chances of this occurring would be greatly increased if there were multiple switches from $B_e = B_g(n)$ to $B_e = B_c(n)$. If we suppose that the process of evolution of culture would begin with n = 0, then natural selection would increase n until the first "local" ESS. Whether it could cross the valley to the globally adap-

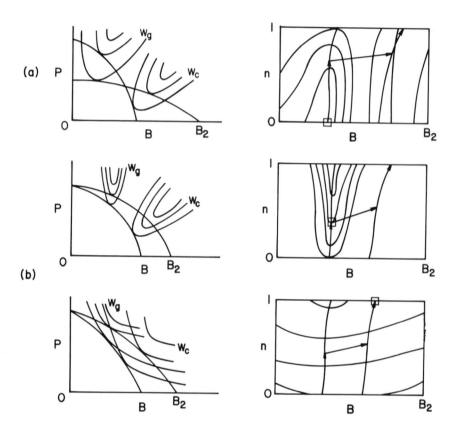

Figure 6.   This figure illustrates two possible evolutionary
    outcomes of the dual inheritance model.   (a) Illustrates
    the case where the capacity for culture has significant
    genetic costs.   Note that the optimal value of W_g de-
    creases as the capacity for culture is increased.   Thus
    the evolutionary stable phenotype has zero capacity for
    culture.   (b) Shows the effect of the steepness of W_g
    on the ESS.   Note that the greater the steepness of W_g
    relative to the distance between W_g and W_c, the greater
    the genetic penalty associated with the culturally
    optimal phenotype and thus the less likely it is to be
    observed.

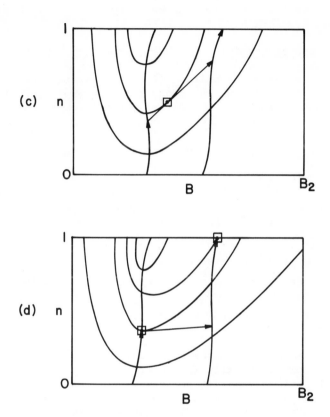

Figure 7.   (a) This figure illustrates that the ESS can lie
   between the genetic and the culturally optimal phenotype.   (b) Illustrates that more than one evolutionary
   stable phenotype is possible.

tive phenotype (in the example shown in 5(d)) would
depend on factors not included in the model, the extent
to which fitness varied in time and space, the extent
to which local populations were isolated and similar
considerations.

The Two-Capacities Model

To incorporate the cultural fitness adjusting mechanisms
of symmetry and bias, we introduce a new parameter, m, that
represents the extent of the direct genetic control of cultural fitness. Thus,

$$W_C = W_C(P, B, m) \tag{6}$$

To simplify the analysis, we will require that the functions
W_g, W_C, and h have the special forms such that for any fixed
value of m the difference in the culturally optimal phenotype, B_C, and the genetically optimal phenotype, B_g, is constant with respect to n, $(\partial B_c/\partial n = 0)$. Call the difference
$B_C - B_g$, ΔB. Thus in this special model ΔB is a unique
measure of the difference between W_g and W_C. Clearly, ΔB is
a function of m. Assume that ΔB is nonnegative and that ΔB
decreases as m decreases $(\partial \Delta B/\partial m = 0)$, thus defining the
units of m.

Also assume that increasing n uniformly makes more fit
organisms (both culturally and genetically) conceivable,
that is the set of possible phenotypes, h, becomes larger as
n increases. Recall that we argued that culture-capacity
will be selected for only when it makes possible genetically
more fit phenotypes. Moreover, it is plausible that for
some traits, notably behavioral ones, that this should be the
case. However, we also assume that as the genetic control
over cultural fitness increases (m → 0) the benefits due to
culture decrease until, when m = 0 and genetic and cultural
fitness are identical ($\Delta B = 0$), there is no benefit to
having culture. This assumption is crucial. The greater
flexibility of cultural inheritance for behaviors requiring
rapid change or extensive geographical specialization is
presumably the cultural system's main adaptive advantage.
In the main text we argued that in order to increase the
coincidence of cultural and genetic fitness, that is, decrease ΔB, genes must increase the detail with which genes
code for "satisfactions" that sift among behavior or restrict
life histories to maintain symmetry. In the limit, to make
cultural and genetic fitness identical, behaviors must be
completely genetically specified; albeit through elaborate,

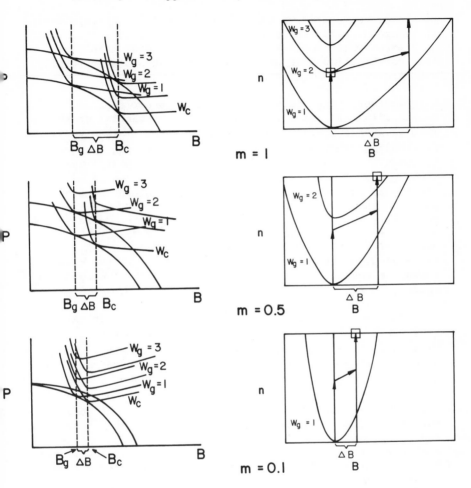

Figure 8. This figure illustrates the graphical solution of
the model extended to allow genetic control of cultural
fitness. The usual graphical determination of the
equilibrium is presented for three values of m, the
parameter that represents the extent of genetic control
of culture. W_g, W_c and h have a special form that results
in B_g being constant and B_c varies only with m. Thus
$B_c - B_g = \Delta B$ provides a unique measure of the effect of
m. As m decreases ΔB decreases. However, so does the
beneficial effect of increasing n on the set of possible
phenotypes. As drawn the genetically optimal value of n
lies between 1 and .1. To find the exact value would
require graphically finding the evolutionarily stable
phenotype for all values of m, and then selecting the
one that maximizes W_g.

intermediate mechanisms of bias and symmetry. In this limit, it seems unreasonable to assume that a separate cultural inheritance system would have any advantage over direct genetic specification of behavior because both would be equally inflexible.

However, this limiting behavior does not preclude the possibility that selection might favor substantial genetic control over W_c, i.e. selection might result in the equilibrium value of m near 0. Consider the following graphical argument. Figure 8 shows the representation of the evolutionary path for three arbitrarily chosen values of m. According to our assumptions, decreasing m should decrease ΔB, thus making the genetic penalty associated with the culturally optimal phenotype smaller. However, decreasing m also decreases the advantages of having a second, cultural system of inheritance. Formally, it reduces the range of phenotypes possible for a given value of n. In the example shown, selection on genes will result in partial genetic control of W_c.

From this argument one can see that some genetical control over W_c will be favored if the initial effect of decreased m is to cause a large reduction on ΔB with a relatively smaller effect on h. Moreover, this seems the likely case. Intuitively, one might suppose that genes can maintain W_c near W_g with some simple genetic controls (broad, basic drives that, for example, make physical comfort and parenthood pleasurable) with little cost in flexibility. On the other hand, it is also clear that complete genetic control will never be favored, no matter what the relative effect of m on B and h, unless the capacity of culture itself is deleterious.

References and Notes

1. M. Sahlins, Culture and Practical Reason (Univ. of
    Chicago Press, Chicago, 1976).
2. C. Darwin, The Descent of Man and Selection in Relation
    to Sex (Murray, London, 1874).
3. R. Fox, in Sexual Selection and the Descent of Man,
    B. Campbell, ed. (Aldine, Chicago, 1972), p. 282; C.D.
    Darlington, The Evolution of Man and Society (Simon and
    Schuster, N.Y., 1969).
4. P.L. Van den Berghe, Man in Society: A Biosocial View
    (Elsevier, N.Y., 1975); W. Irons, in Evolutionary
    Biology and Human Social Behavior: An Anthropological
    Perspective, W.A. Chagnon and W. Irons, eds. (Duxbury,
    N. Scituate, Mass., 1979), p. 4.
5. E.O. Wilson, Sociobiology (Harvard, Cambridge, 1975).
6. E.O. Wilson, Deadalus 27, 127 (1977) and On Human
    Nature (Harvard Univ. Press, Cambridge, 1978).
7. M. Sahlins (1) and The Use and Abuse of Biology (Univ.
    Michigan Press, Ann Arbor, 1976).
8. T. Dobzhansky, Mankind Evolving: The Evolution of the
    Human Species (Yale Univ. Press, New Haven, 1962).
9. R.M. Keesing, Ann. Rev. Anthrop. 3, 73 (1974).
10. R. Lewontin, The Genetic Basis of Evolutionary Change
    (Columbia Univ. Press, N.Y., 1974).
11. A. Rapoport, Sci. Am. 217, 50 (1967).
12. P.J. Richerson, Human Ecology 6, 117 (1978).
13. J. Maynard-Smith, Ann. Rev. of Ecol. and Syst. 9, 31
    (1978).
14. R. LeVine, Culture, Behavior and Personality: An In-
    troduction to the Comparative Study of Psychosocial
    Adaptation (Aldine, Chicago, 1973); T.L. Rosenthal and
    B.J. Zimmerman, Social Learning and Cognition (Academic
    Press, N.Y., 1978).
15. A.R. Jensen, Educability and Group Differences (Basic
    Books, N.Y., 1973); R.T. Osborne, C.E. Noble and
    N. Weyl, eds. Human Variation: The Biopsychology of
    Age, Race and Sex (Academic Press, N.Y., 1978).
16. L.L. Cavalli-Sforza and M.W. Feldman, Genetics 40, 391
    (1978); P. Lewontin and M.W. Feldman, Science 190,
    1163 (1975).
17. S. Scarr Salapatek, Science 174, 1285 (1971); Science
    174, 1223 (1971); S. Scarr and R.A. Weinberg Am.
    Psychol. 31, 726 (1976); S. Scarr, in this volume.
18. D.T. Campbell, in: Social Change in Developing Areas
    H.R. Barringer, G.I. Blanksten and R.W. Mach, eds.
    (Schenkman, Cambridge, 1965), p. 19 and Am. Psychol.
    30, 1103 (1975).
19. H.R. Pulliam and C. Dunford, Programmed to Learn: An
    Essay on the Evolution of Culture (Columbia Univ. Press,

N.Y., 1980); M.W. Feldman and L.L. Cavalli-Sforza, Theor. Pop. Biol. 9, 238 (1976); F.T. Cloak, Human Ecology 3, 161 (1975); R. Dawkins, The Selfish Gene (Oxford Univ. Press, N.Y., 1976); P.J. Richerson and R. Boyd, J. Soc. Biol. Structures 1, 127 (1978).

20. C.J. Bajema, Eugen. Quart. 10, 175 (1963).
21. C. Levi-Strauss, The Savage Mind (Univ. of Chicago Press, Chicago, 1966).
22. F.T. Cloak (19).
23. Feldman and Cavalli-Sforza (19).
24. Slatkin, M. PNAS (U.S.A.) 66, 87 (1970); J. Rocklin and G. Oster, J. Math. Biol. 3, 225 (1976); S. Sterns, Ann. Rev. Ecol. and Syst. 8, 145 (1977); G. Oster and E.O. Wilson Caste and Ecology in the Social Insects (Princeton Univ. Press, Princeton, 1978) Ch. 8 and J. Maynard-Smith (13).
25. H.R. Pulliam, personal communication.
26. N. Bischof, in Biosocial Anthropology, R. Fox, ed. (Wiley, N.Y., 1975), p. 37.
27. J. Maynard-Smith, Am. Sci. 64, 41 (1976).
28. R. Boyd and P.J. Richerson, Multiple Parents and Non-linear Cultural Transmission, in preparation.
29. K. Flannery, Ann. Rev. Anthrop. 2, 271 (1973).
30. Richerson and Boyd (19).
31. W.H. Durham, Human Ecology 4, 89 (1976) and Quart. Rev. Biol. 51, 385 (1978) in The Sociobiology Debate A.L. Caplan, ed. (Harper, N.Y., 1978), p. 428.
32. W.H. Durham, (31) (1978).
33. Ibid.
34. H.D. Fishbein, Evolution, Development and Children's Learning (Goodyear, Pacific Palisades, 1976).
35. See also P.A. Corning, in Evolutionary Biology 7, 253, T. Dobzhansky, M. Hecht and W.C. Steere eds. (Plenum Press, N.Y., 1973); R.D. Alexander and G. Borgia, Ann. Rev. Ecol. Syst. 9, 449 (1978).
36. Dobzhansky (8); Wilson (5); Keesing (9); C. Geertz, in Theories of the Mind, J. Scher ed. (MacMillan, N.Y., 1962), p. 713.
37. Pulliam and Dunford (19).
38. Geertz (36).
39. C.D. Darlington (3) and in Osborne et al. (15).
40. T. Dobzhansky, in Evolutionary Throught in America S. Persons ed. (Yale Univ. Press, New Haven, 1950), p. 86.
41. Wilson (6).
42. Wilson (5) pp. 381-382.
43. Alexander and Borgia (35).
44. R.D. Alexander, in Evolutionary Biology and Human Social Behavior: An Anthropological Perspective. N.A. Chagnon

and W. Irons eds. (Duxbury, N. Scituate, Mass., 1979), p. 59.
45. B.G.J. Galef, Adv. Study Behavior 6, 77 (1976).
46. Galef (45); K. Immelman in Function and Evolution in Behavior, Essays in Honor of Niko Tinbergen (Clarendon, Oxford, 1975); J. Itani and A. Nishimura, in Precultural Primate Behavior, E.W. Mexzel ed. (S. Kruger, Basel, 1973), p. 26.
47. J. Maynard-Smith, Quart. Rev. Biol. 51, 277 (1975).
48. T.L. Jinks, Extra Chromosomal Inheritance (Prentice Hall, Englewood Cliffs, N.J., 1964); C.W. Birky, Bioscience 26, 26 (1976).
49. K.W. Butzer, Environment and Archeology: An Ecological Approach to Prehistory (Aldine, Chicago, 1971), p. 18.
50. S.L. Washburn, Sci. Am. 253, 62 (1960); C.J. Jolly, Man (n.s.) 5, 5 (1970).
51. D.C. Johanson and T.D. White, Science 203, 321 (1979); M.D. Leaky, National Geographic 155, 446 (1979); F.C. Howell, in The Evolution of African Mammals, V.J. Maglio and H.B.S. Cooke, eds. (Harvard Univ. Press, Cambridge, 1978), p. 154.
52. G.L. Isaac, Ann. N.Y. Acad. Sci. 280, 275 (1976).
53. N.J. Shackelton and N.D. Opdyke, in Investigation of Late Quaternary Paleoceanography and Paleoclimatology R.D. Cline and J.D. Hays, eds., Geological Soc. of American Memoir No. 145, (1976), p. 449.
54. N.J. Shackelton and N.D. Opdyke, Quat. Res. 3, 39 (1973); D.A. Livingstone, Ann. Rev. Ecol. Syst. 6, 249 (1975).
55. J. Piaget, Biology and Knowledge, (Univ. of Chicago Press, Chicago, 1971); C.E. Laughlin, Jr. and E.G. d'Aquili, Biogenic Structuralism (Columbia Univ. Press, N.Y., 1974); and Fishbein (34).
56. Rosenthal and Zimmerman (14).
57. LeVine (14).
58. P. Marler and S. Peters, Science 189, 519 (1977).
59. Galef (46), Itani and Nishimura (46).
60. Itani and Nishimura (46).
61. J. Steward, Theory of Culture Change: The Methodology of Multilinear Evolution (Univ. of Illinois Press, Urbana, 1955); F. Barth, Models of Social Organization Anthrop. Inst. Occasional Paper 23, 33 (1966); B.S. Orlove, Cultural Ecology: A Critical Essay and Bibliography (Institute of Ecology Publication No. 13, Univ. of California Davis, Davis, Calif., 1977).
62. E. Mayr, Animal Species and Evolution (Harvard Univ. Press, Cambridge, 1963); J. Endler, Geographic Variation, Speciation and Clines (Princeton University Press, Princeton, N.J., 1977).

63. Mayr (62); S.M. Stanley PNAS (U.S.A.) 72, 645 (1975).
64. H.C. Carson, Am. Natur. 109, 83 (1975).
65. R. Naroll and R. Wirsting, J. Conflict Resolution 20, 187 (1976).
66. P. Liberman, On the Origins of Language (MacMillan, N.Y., 1975).
67. N. Chomsky, Ann. N.Y. Acad. Sci. 280, 46 (1976).
68. W.D. Hamilton, J. Theor. Biol. 7, 1 (1964); L.L. Cavalli-Sforza and M.W. Feldman, Theor. Pop. Biol. 14, 268 (1978); S. Yokoyama and J. Felsenstein, PNAS (U.S.A.) 75, 420 (1978); M. Wade, PNAS (U.S.A.) 75, 6154 (1978).
69. Sahlins (7) 1976.
70. P.L. Van den Berghe and D. Barash, Amer. Anthrop. 74, 809 (1977).
71. R. Fox, Kinship and Marriage (Penguin, London, 1967); R.M. Keesing, Kin Groups and Social Structure (Holt, Reinhardt and Winston, N.Y., 1975).
72. For patrilineal systems see: J. Hartung, Current Anthrop. 17, 607 (1975); M. Dickeman, Paternal Confidence and Dowry Competition: A biocultural analysis of purdah, Presented to Symposium on Natural Selection and Social Behavior, Ann Arbor, (Oct. 1978). For matrilineal systems see, P.J. Greene, Am. Ethnologist 5, 151 (1978); R.D. Alexander in Changing Scenes in the Natural Sciences 1776-1976 Academy of Natural Sciences Special Pub. 12, p. 283; J. Kurland in Chagnon and Irons (31), p. 135.
73. G.C. Williams, Adaptation and Natural Selection (Princeton Univ. Press, Princeton, N.J., 1966).
74. Richerson and Boyd, unpublished m.s. See also Richerson and Boyd (19) and Pulliam and Dunford (19).
75. G.C. Williams, Sex and Evolution (Princeton Univ. Press, Princeton, N.J., 1975).
76. M. Dickeman, P.J. Greene and R.D. Alexander (72).
77. M. Dickeman (72).
78. C.F. Sing, D.C. Sheffler, J.V. Neel and J.A. Napier, Hum. Genet. 23, 150 (1971); E. Peritz and P.F. Rust, Amer. J. Hum. Genet. 24, 46 (1972).
79. J.V. Neel and K.M. Weiss, The genetic structure of a tribal population, the Yanomamo Indians, Am. J. Phys. Anthrop. 42, 25 (1975); N. Chagnon, Yanomamo: The Fierce People (Holt, Reinhardt and Winston, N.Y., 1969).
80. G.P. Murdock, Social Structure (MacMillan, N.Y., 1949) and Ethnographic Atlas (Univ. of Pittsburg Press, Pittsburg, 1967).
81. For a discussion of such constraints see Stearns (24) and Oster and Wilson (24).
82. J. Hirshleifer, J. Law. Econ. 20, 1 (1977).

Margaret S. Collins, Irving W. Wainer,
Theodore A. Bremner

Conclusion

 K⎸⟨ ⌐ Background of the Symposium

During the last decade, there has been a resurgence of
racism in America of an intensity nearly equalling that seen
here during the years 1900 to 1920. An educational psychologist, Arthur Jensen, has resurrected the long-abandoned idea
that Black/White differences in performance on IQ tests are
primarily the result of differential genetic endowments.[1] A
physicist, William Shockley, maintains that people are color-
coded for intelligence and success, such that the darker one
is, the less intellectually and socially able he could be expected to be. [2] Similar views are shared by the psychologists
Richard Herrnstein and H.J. Eysenck. [3]

These ideas were attacked promptly and vigorously by a
number of able scientists (Lewontin, Feldman, Layzer, Kamin,
others)[4], who pointed out that these ideas betrayed not only
a lack of understanding of basic genetics, but also that the
proponents were using heritability measures improperly.
Throughout Jensen's investigations there seems to have been a
failure to appreciate the complexity of the environment in
which development of cognitive skills takes place. / This conflict has been chronicled by Allen, who considered the responses of the scientific community to racist ideas during the
period 1900-1920, and contrasted these responses to the speed
and vigor with which current geneticists and other scientists
pointed out the flaws in the hereditarian position taken by
Jensen and his followers.[5] While the earlier geneticists
came to deplore the excesses of the eugenicists that led to
the drastic immigration policies enacted during the twenties,
they were far less inclined to take a public position against
the proponents of eugenics than the geneticists of today are
in opposing racism. The usual practice then was to withdraw
from the eugenics movement quietly, after data revealed the

154 Collins et al.

factual and methodological weaknesses of the eugenics movement. Notable exceptions existed, however, and toward the
middle twenties, several distinguished scientists, H.S. Jen-
nings, Raymond Pearl, E.M. East, and W.E. Castle, publicly re-
pudiated the racist propaganda of the eugenicists and offered
biological refutations. Somewhat later, Theodosius Dobzhansky
collaborated with an anthropologist, W. Ashley Montagu, and
together they laid to rest the doctrine of racial superiority.[6] The events during this period have been summarized and
analyzed by Cravens.[7]

Geneticists today are fairly well agreed on certain aspects of inheritance in man as it relates to racial differences and especially IQ measures. The position is well summarized in McClearn's paper presented to the XII International Congress of Genetics in 1969.[8] A very detailed, well
documented and readable account of this position has been
done by Ehrlich and Feldman .[9]

A brief summary of the position as it now appears to be
among modern geneticists follows:

1. The extent of variation within any human population
   generally far exceeds the average difference between
   two populations for features influenced by multiple
   genes. This has been found to be true for performance
   on many standardized IQ tests, where scores of Black/
   White samples overlap almost completely over a wide
   spread, while average differences between the two
   groups are relatively small.

2. Interpreting these average differences as evidence of
   genetic differences is unjustified, since the samples
   include individuals of diverse environmental back-
   grounds and all the available evidence shows that factors such as nutrition, environmental complexity,so-
   cioeconomic status, and additional factors as yet un-
   defined may influence test performance.

3. IQ tests are usually standardized for only one group
   of the groups being compared ; further, they are tests
   of achieved, rather than innate, ability and are culture dependent.

4. Races in man are social rather than biological entities.

5. Estimates of IQ heritability do not provide useful information on the causes of phenotypic differences in
   man.

Jensen had drawn much support for his ideas initially from the work of Sir Cyril Burt, an English psychologist whose work has recently been shown to suffer from methodological flaws of such magnitude as to render his conclusions valueless in a scientific exercise.[7] In spite of the lack of objective data in support of Jensen's and Shockley's arguments, they have received much favorable press coverage, and at least some state and national policies have been influenced by them.[9] Jensen was elected a fellow of the Psychology section of the AAAS in 1977, after heated discussion.

This adherence to a set of ideas lacking in adequate factual basis by contemporary scholars, and the marked differences in publicizing the two sides of the arguments centering around Jensen suggested the desirability of an additional treatment, marshalling some of the evidence available to scientists who view this issue from a different perspective. AAAS sponsorship made a symposium possible ; this volume is an outgrowth of that symposium.

The symposium contributors considered several aspects of the problem, including factors affecting the subjective analysis of data; how data are utilized by non-scientists; the question of the biological reality of the concept of race in man; the impact of the culture on particular human features; and finally, a model proposed to permit analysis of the role of genetic and cultural factors in influencing the direction of human diversification.

Summary and Analysis

There are a number of approaches to the nature/nurture controversy. One approach concerns itself with factors affecting the subjective analysis of data. Such factors include the interaction between cultural, economic and political phenomena on the one hand, and scientific research and thought on the other. This interaction occurs in the individual scientist, who is a product of society and who reflects trends of that society in the understanding and utilization of scientific data and theory. This aspect of the problem and its impact on the question of human equality is highlighted by the contributions of Moore, Gropper, and Baba and Darga.

Moore's examination of the interaction between Herbert Spencer and Andrew Carnegie begins with the caveat that "we are much less interested in what Herbert Spencer actually said and wrote than in what he was understood to have said ..." Moore then goes on to demonstrate how Carnegie incorporates and molds Spencer's work into his own partisan socio-

logical views, views which reflect the inherently unequal
relationship between Carnegie and the emerging American upper
class on the one hand, and the middle and working classes,
minorities, eastern European immigrants, and women on the
other. Carnegie's "scientific" theory justifying inequality
was a direct descendant of the philosophy of the slaveholder.

While the Spencer/Carnegie example typifies how science
interacts with social theory, Moore is also interested in the
reverse effect: how society colors scientific thought and
research. He investigates the socialization of young Americans through football, Junior Achievement, and Boy Scouts.
These activities develop the subjective framework which will
eventually be used to analyze objective data and develop
scientific theory. The cycle Science → Social Theory → Socialization → Science has been set in motion. Thus, it is
not surprising to Moore that Carnegie's social theories continue to reappear.

Moore's thesis was supported and expanded by Stephan
Chorover's presentation "Behind the Golden Door: The Politics of Defining, Measuring, and Controlling the Contents of
the American Melting Pot." This paper has been published
elsewhere (Chapter 4 in From Genesis to Genocide, MIT Press,
1979), but some of his ideas will be summarized here. Chorover raised the question of cultural bias in scientific investigation. Using the example of measuring intelligence on
the basis of whether the individual being measured is more
or less ape-like, Chorover asked the question "How does the
investigator choose which characteristic to use in his investigation ?" If one chose to compare Europeans and Africans
to the chimpanzee and gorilla, and further chose hair as the
factor to be compared, it can be shown that on the basis of
hair caliber, the African is "closer to the apes". However,
if the amount and distribution of body hair are used as the
measure, Europeans are clearly "closer to the apes". The
choice is not objective, it is subjective, and depends upon
how the scientist has been socialized and how he views the
world.

Stephen Jay Gould has discussed this same point in a recent article on Samuel George Morton's ranking of human intelligence on the basis of cranial capacity.[10] In his article , Gould points out that Morton was predisposed to the
conclusion that Anglo-Americans were intellectually superior
to Indians, who were, in turn, superior to Africans. Morton
then manipulated and analyzed his data in such a manner as to
support his views, and in so doing, carried his social biases
into his scientific work. His work could be used to train
other scientists.

It is of interest to observe that Moore, Chorover and Gould represent a section of the American scientific community whose socialization includes not only football, Monopoly and Boy Scouts, but also the recent civil rights and anti-war movements. They have broken away from the Spencer/Carnegie cycle and are attempting to redefine and reestablish the science/society cycle in a different manner.

Baba and Darga's paper, "The Genetic Myth of Racial Classification," is an overview of the development of scientific theories of race and how they are affected by the prevailing social structure. In their view, prevailing political and economic inequalities of various national-ethnic groupings are the root of most "scientific" racial taxonomies. And further, most of these racial theories are developed far beyond what was originally intended by their authors. Such over-extension is an example of the kind of situation Moore warned against when he cautioned that one should be cognizant of how a scientific theory is understood and applied.

The papers of Scarr and Zegura consider different aspects of the nature/nurture problem and document the impact of the culture and specific social environment on particular features, viz. biochemical characteristics and performance on IQ tests. Free of the bias so prominent in the works of those hereditarians apparently seeking to justify preservation of social inequalities, these papers exemplify an enlightened approach to the problem of human cultural evolution.

Richerson and Boyd focus on possible mechanisms of human evolution, and propose a dual inheritance model in which both genetic and cultural factors influence the direction of human diversification. Like other authors in this volume, they recognize the importance of environmental factors in phenotype determination, but, additionally, they offer a feedback model which may answer many of the questions posed by sociobiologists.

If this summary focusses on only a few of the many aspects of this volume, it is because the editors feel that the messages included in these sections are an answer and a challenge to the scientific community and to society as a whole. Bias exists and is pervasive—but we must somehow minimize the intrusion of bias in studies of man and his institutions. We need to understand the dynamics of the interaction between science and society, the forces which are involved, and the procedures necessary to train more scientists who are aware of the unavoidable biases attendant upon the acculturation process and who are capable of structuring their investigations in such a fashion as to negate these biases.

These caveats have been expressed by others, especially in recent years. However, the recent resurgence of racism and the emphasis given to hereditarian explanations of human differences suggested that the caveats should be restated.

References

1. A. Jensen, Harvard Educational Review 39:2 (1969); Psychology Today, Dec. (1973).

2. W. Shockley, in: N. Daniels, Harper's 247:25 (1973).

3. R. Herrnstein, Atlantic Monthly, Sept. (1971) p 58-59 H.J. Eysenck, The IQ Argument (Library Press, Freeport, N.Y., 1971).

4. R. Lewontin, Ann. Rev. Genetics, (1975); Evol. Biol. 4:381-388, (1967); Bull. Atomic Sci., March, (1970) p 2-8; M. Feldman and R. Lewontin, Science 190, No. 4220, p 1163-1168 (1975); D. Layzer, Science 183, No. 4131 (1974) p 1259-66; L. Kamin, Science and Politics of IQ, (New York, Wiley) 1974.

5. G.E. Allen, Genetics 79:29-45 (Suppl. Part 2, 1975).

6. T. Dobzhansky and M. Ashley-Montagu, Science 105 (1947) p 590.

7. H. Cravens, The Triumph of Evolution, (Univ. Penn. Press, 1978).

8. G. McClearn, Proc. XII Inter. Cong. Genetics 3:419-30 (1969).

9. P. Ehrlich and S. Feldman, The Race Bomb, (Ballantine Books, 1977).

10. S. Gould, Science 200 (4341):503-509. (1978).